LOCOMOTION PAPERS   LP175

The
INGLETON BRANCH
A Lost Route to Scotland

by
Robert Western

THE OAKWOOD PRESS

© Robert Western, 2018

ISBN 978-0-85361-446-3

First Edition published as The Lowgill Branch 1971
Second Edition 1990
Third Edition 2018

Printed by P2D Books, 1 Newlands Rd,
Westoning, Bedford, MK45 5LD

By the same author

The Cockermouth, Keswick & Penrith Railway
The Coniston Railway
The Eden Valley Railway
The Kendal & Windermere Railway

All published by the Oakwood Press.

Author's Note

When the first edition of this history of the line from Ingleton to Lowgill (and also to include at the appropriate stage the section to Clapham) was written in 1969 and published in 1971, it carried the title *The Lowgill Branch*. This was incorrect and came about as the result of a postal strike! Unlike today when communication is so very easy, this block led to the publisher having to decide the title. In fact, the line was never known as 'The Lowgill Branch'. At various times it was 'The Orton Branch'and 'The Lune Valley Line' but in the end was given the official title 'The Ingleton Branch'.

The spelling of Lowgill has been kept to one word as shown on the Ordnance Survey maps, although 'railway company' spellings have shown Low Gill as two words.

Published by
The Oakwood Press, 54-58 Mill Square, Catrine, KA5 6RD
Telephone: 01290 551122   Website: www.stenlake.co.uk

Contents

The Prologue 5
Chapter One   Beginnings: 1845 to 1855 7
    The North Western Railway. A Scheme to link the West
    Riding with the North West. A Bill and subsequent Act.
    Some modifications. The NWR opens. Some further
    negotiations.
Chapter Two   Rival Schemes: 1855 to 1857 15
    Problems. The Lancaster and Carlisle Railway steps in.
    The Commons Committee makes a decision.
Chapter Three   Construction: 1858 to 1861 27
    The contracts. Some developments in company politics.
    The line opens.
An Interlude   A journey down the line 37
Chapter Four   Relegation to a Rural Branch: 1862 to 1876 39
    The Sedbergh – Hawes Railway.
    The Midland decides to go it alone.
    Richard Moon steps in.
    Relegation to a rural branch.
Chapter Five   The Quiet Years Begin: 1876 to 1920 53
    Serving the rural community.
    The Lake District Express.
    A royal visit.
Chapter Six   A Further Period of Change: 1920 to 1948 67
    The 'Big Four'. The Second World War.
    Nationalization of Britain's Railway System.
Chapter Seven   Decline and Closure: 1948 to 1967 79
    A vital choice is made.
    The last passenger train.
    A celebration with a tinge of sadness.
    A little respite. The end of the line.
Chapter Eight   A Review of Motive Power on the Branch 87
Chapter Nine   After Closure 93
    Some preservation and what remains.
Appendix 1   Bills affecting the Ingleton Branch 95
Appendix 2   Some significant dates 96
Appendix 3   Bridges and viaducts 99
Sources 103
Acknowledgements 104

A view from 'The Lincolnshire Poacher' as it heads northwards over the Lune viaduct on the Ingleton branch with locomotive class 'V2', No. 60870 in charge on 17th June, 1962.
J.R. Sugden

Prologue

The best view of the imposing northern end of the Ingleton Railway Branch is from the top of Winder Fell, just outside Sedbergh. From here, some 1,500ft above sea level, the branch can be seen sweeping away from the main line at Lowgill, over the Lowgill viaduct and through the Lune Valley, across the River Lune and River Rawthey viaducts and away along the side of the Barbon Fells towards Kirkby Lonsdale. The fact that the track is no longer in place makes little difference to this view of the line and if the viewer did not have the good fortune to travel along this scenic branch, then something of its former glory can be experienced from this high vantage point.

The Ingleton branch was the bone of contention between several railway companies for many years.

From its outset when its construction was planned by the North Western Railway Company, in 1846, the intentions of that company were bedevilled by lack of money and the scheming of other companies. As a result, this short section of line (only about 18 miles in length) became a significant missing link in the attempt to make a through route from London to Scotland, via the West Riding of Yorkshire.

The following account recalls the events which first led to a line which remained in the planning stage for 11 years and then, even when built, failed to serve the purpose for which it was originally intended; namely to form part of a main line from London to Scotland.

When considering these events, it is necessary to bear in mind the powerful and often ruthless background influence of the London and North Western Railway. This company, formed in 1846 from The London and Birmingham Railway, the already amalgamated Grand Junction and Liverpool and Manchester railways, the Manchester and Birmingham Railway and others already absorbed into these, had control of a larger section of the route from London (Euston) to Carlisle than any other individual company. (From Carlisle to Glasgow the Caledonian Railway originally operated this section.)

The London and North Western Railway was inclined to play 'big brother' to the smaller constituent companies sharing the route, including the Lancaster and Carlisle Railway, and eventually gained control of the whole line from Euston to Carlisle.

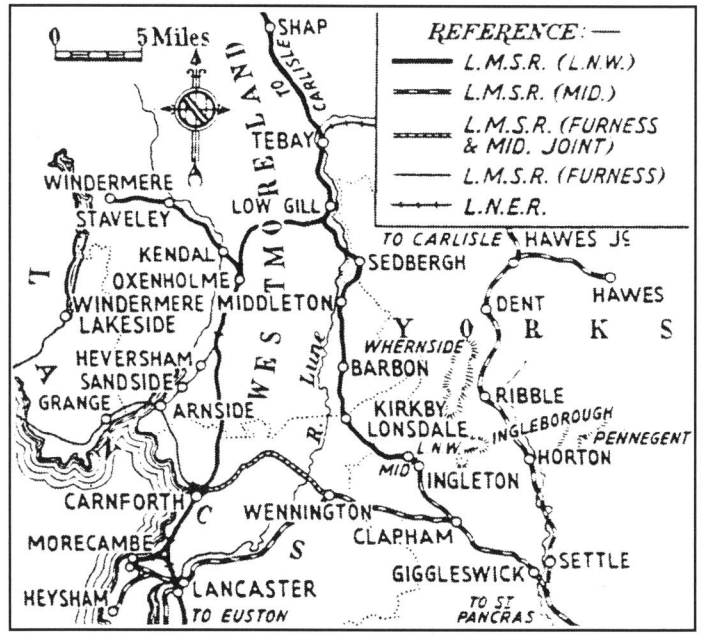

Map showing the Ingleton branch of the LMSR.

Map showing the southbound spur and the two deviations proposed.

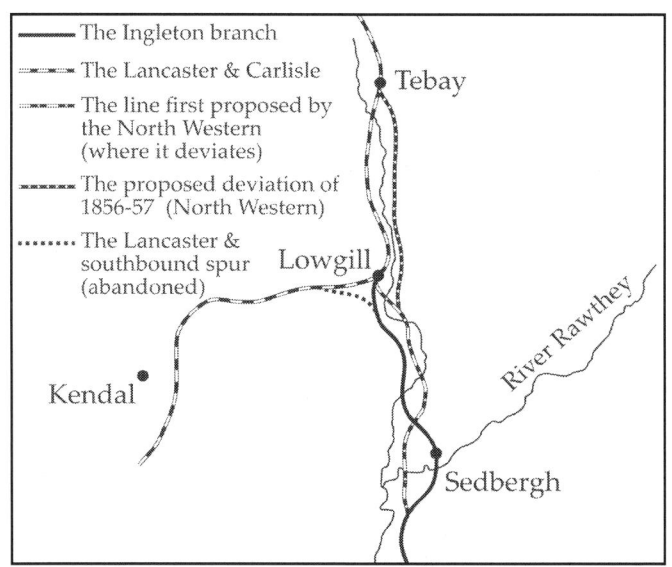

Chapter One

Beginnings
1845 to 1855

1845

The saga of the Ingleton Branch has its beginnings in 1845. In that year the Lancaster and Carlisle Railway (L&C) was engaged in building the line between the places named in the company's title. This line, once completed, would extend the London to Scotland rail link from Euston, leaving only the section from Carlisle to Scotland to be completed. This section would be undertaken by the Caledonian Railway (CR).

Also in this year, the Leeds and Bradford Railway (L&B) successfully applied to Parliament for an Act to build an extension from its line to Shipley, northwards, to Skipton and Colne. Once the Bill received the Royal Assent, work started immediately.

In the circumstances, this situation offered good potential for a further scheme to link the L&B extension line through the West Riding, in a north-westerly direction, to the L&C line, thereby effecting a route from Leeds to Carlisle and, once the Carlisle to Glasgow section had been completed, to Scotland.

With such a link in view, a provisional committee for a company to be called the North Western Railway Company (NWR) issued its Prospectus and scheme in February.

The Scheme

Charles Vignoles and Robert Stephenson were responsible for preparing the plan for the railway.

In its proposed form, it was in four sections.

The first was for a main line from the L&B line to the L&C line. This would leave the L&B just outside Skipton and pass through Ingleton and Kirkby Lonsdale before joining the L&C at Rowell Green, near Heversham.

The second section was for a short branch from the main line. This was known as the Sedgwick Branch. It would leave the main line near Nook and pass north-westwards to join the L&C at Raynes Hall, at Sedgwick. The branch was to be about four miles long.

The next section dealt with a plan for another branch from the main line which would leave the latter near Wenning Bridge and go to Saint

George's Quay at Lancaster. It was referred to, appropriately, as the Lancaster Branch.

The fourth and final section of the proposals was the one which has the most relevance for this account. It proposed a branch from the main line near Casterton, which would join the L&C near Scufton House, not far from Lowgill. The line was referred to as the Orton Branch.

With these proposals in view, the L&B Company was approached and negotiations were held in an attempt to reach an agreement on the matter of a junction with its line near Skipton. A settlement was reached whereby the NWR allocated to the L&B 16,000 shares in the company and all the Directors of the L&B became Directors of the NWR.

As far as the northern junction with the L&C was concerned, there seems to have been no difficulty with a settlement. The L&C stood to benefit from the traffic which would pass onto its line from the West Riding. In fact, the L&C went even further than simply accepting the NWR proposals. It agreed to be responsible for building the section of line from Up Hall, near Casterton, to its own line at Scufton House.

1846–1848
The NWR Bill gets the Royal Assent

On the 26th June 1846, the NWR Bill received the Royal Assent, but with considerable modifications. Sections 1 and 2 were deleted. These included the original main line through Kirkby Lonsdale to the L&C at Rowell Green. As a result, the main line was now taken as the Orton Branch (Section 4 of the original scheme) and the Lancaster line became a branch of this. The Act was described as 'An Act for making a railway from the Leeds and Bradford Extension Railway to the Lancaster and Carlisle Railway with a diverging line therefrom to Lancaster to be called the North Western Railway'.

Some sections of the Bill are worthy of special note as they affect later issues. Section 46 concerns the transfer of the section of line from Up Hall, northwards, to the L&C. It stated that it would be lawful for the company, with the approbation of three-fifths of the votes of the proprietors present, either personally or by proxy, at some General Meeting, convened for the purpose, 'to sell or transfer to the Lancaster and Carlisle, with its agreement, the section of the line between Up Hall and the junction with the Lancaster and Carlisle, whether completed or not'. As will be seen, the NWR later tried to revoke this condition and this gave rise to indignant protests from the L&C.

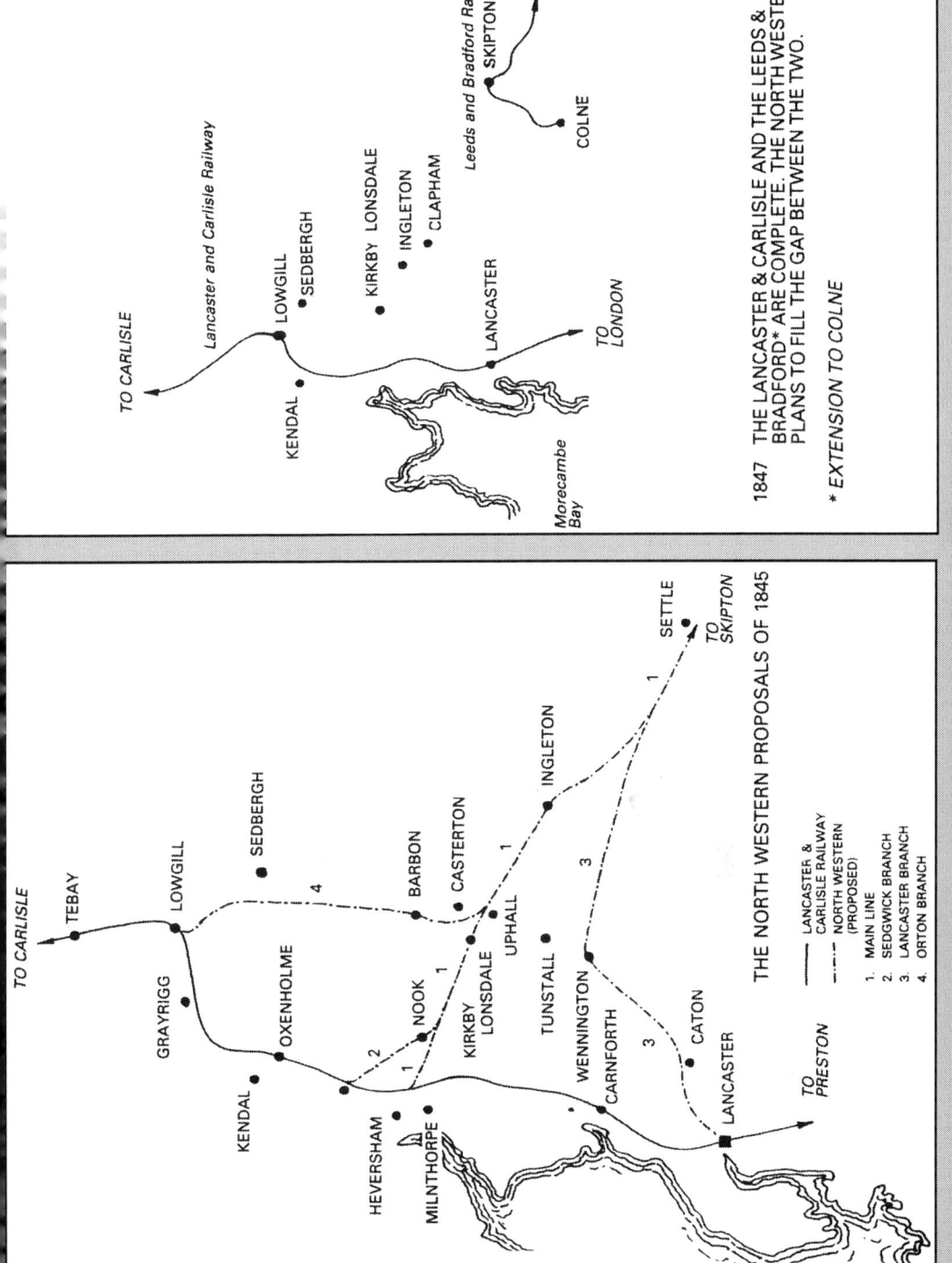

Section 50 involves the NWR in an undertaking not to 'prejudice or diminish any of the Rights, Powers or Privileges of the Lancaster and Carlisle'. This, too, would be a point at issue some years later.

Originally the line from Up Hall was to pass to the west of High Casterton, through Low Casterton and to the east of Barbon. It would then continue northwards crossing the River Lune at Waterside, just south of the church in Firbank.

In 1846 and 1848 plans were deposited for deviations. The first was to be at Casterton, where it was intended to take the line to the east of both High and Low Casterton. The second was to be near Sedbergh, where the line would sweep eastwards in a wide arc to approach nearer this market town. This latter proposal was, in effect, despite further modifications, almost identical to the route taken by the line when it was eventually built. The change in the vicinity of Sedbergh resulted in a plan to run the line east of the River Lune, through Howgill (by the woollen mill) and then over the Lune at Midge Hole, near Dillicar.

In July 1846, the first general meeting of the NWR shareholders was held at The Kings Arms in Lancaster. The Directors outlined the scheme and pointed out that the L&C would be responsible for building the line from Up Hall to the junction near Dillicar.

Something of a set back to the scheme came only three months later when, in October, the L&C, having virtually completed its line, decided against building the Orton Branch, so throwing the responsibility back onto the NWR. On the last day of 1846, at a ceremony at Cleatop, near Settle, the first sod was cut by Lord Morpeth, a Member of Parliament for the West Riding. Reports describe how he dressed up for the part in a navvy's attire, much to the amusement of the crowd, in a period when antics of that sort were by no means commonplace. Despite the very cold weather, the festivities went well and it would have been difficult to foretell at the time that the NWR would soon be facing considerable problems.

In July 1847, the Ingleton contract was awarded to the firm of Coulthard and Allen for £108,000 and work began. However, the scheme did not proceed as anticipated. By the end of the year the NWR began to feel the stringency of the money market, prevalent at the time in railway circles. Forced into cutting expenditure, the NWR started to look for suitable places where it could exercise economy. After consultation with Stephenson it was decided, in August 1848, to discontinue work on the Ingleton to Lowgill section and press for completion of the line to Lancaster.

This decision was not really a surprising one. The heavy earthworks and bridges needed on the Ingleton to Lowgill section would involve considerable cost and by deciding not to proceed beyond Ingleton some £350,000 would be saved. So, at the end of 1848 all that existed of the Orton Branch was a single track up to Ingleton and the foundations for the viaduct which it had been intended would span the River Greta, north of the town. The NWR had purchased plots of land almost as far as Cowan Bridge but there, for the time being, proposals had to rest. Coulthard and Allen turned their efforts from north of Ingleton to the Lancaster line. Several years later they would return to the Orton Branch, although not for the NWR.

1849

At the half-yearly meeting of the NWR shareholders in August 1849, which was held in Skipton, the company announced that a service between Skipton and Ingleton had commenced. The work carried out north of Ingleton before the decision was made to abandon that section had cost £18,500 but the view was expressed that this loss was better justified than the further expenditure needed to complete the Orton Branch.

1850
The NWR opens

At the half-yearly meeting of the L&C in March, the Chairman, E.W. Hassel informed the shareholders of an agreement whereby the NWR would be provided with accommodation at Lancaster Station. This would make it possible for travellers from the West Riding and the Midlands, who were travelling to Scotland, to make a connection at Lancaster.

On Saturday 1st June, 1850, on the completion of the section of the line between Bentham and Clapham, the NWR line from Skipton to Lancaster opened. Five trains ran each way daily and as a result of an agreement with the Midland Company, which had by this time taken over the L&B, the NWR passengers could be conveyed from Leeds and Bradford to Lancaster without having to change.

This arranged, the Orton Branch seemed to lose its importance and the line from Clapham to Ingleton was closed to traffic. Possibly one of the first closures in branch line history.

Interest from another quarter.

Closed though it was, the matter did not rest there. In the background another railway company had rapidly been gaining ground and was thinking in terms of a route to Scotland. This company was the Great Northern Railway (GNR). Back in 1848 it was already running trains from Kings Cross to Askern on its own line and then over the Manchester and Leeds (renamed the Lancashire and Yorkshire Railway) to Methley and from there, over the rails of the Midland Railway (MR) into Leeds. The GNR planned to take a line from Askern to York and make connections there for Scotland.

However the River Tyne and the River Tweed still needed bridges and so the GNR looked for an alternative route. At this point it turned its attention to the Orton Branch because, if constructed, this line of railway would provide a missing link in what would be the shortest route from London to Scotland and the GNR, working with the MR and the companies beyond Leeds, could well provide stiff competition with the route from Euston. However the MR could not agree to a scheme whereby it and the GNR would both provide capital to build the branch and negotiations between these two companies lapsed as a result.

Perhaps this move, with its subsequent failure, prompted the NWR to revive plans to build the Orton Branch and in an attempt to find a backer, the company turned to the L&C. The time seemed right because during this period the L&C and London & North Western Railway (LNWR) were not on the best of terms. It seems that the L&C objected to the power the LNWR exerted in the policies of the west coast main line running. Coupled with this was the fact that LNWR and MR had been considering amalgamation and so the L&C felt that its ally was perhaps to be found in the GNR. For a while it looked as though the L&C and the GNR might construct the branch but these plans also came to nothing.

1852

By 1852 the NWR, realizing that construction of the branch was something of a remote possibility, made application to Parliament and was granted an extension for the completion time for another five years. The agreement to lease or sell the section of the branch from Up Hall to the L&C was reaffirmed and this was to become a vital issue only four years later when the latter company opposed further schemes which the NWR put forward.

1853–1855
Further Negotiations

During the next three years a good deal of discussion and negotiation between various companies ensued which either centred upon or affected in some way, the Orton Branch. The companies at various stages were the NWR, MR, L&C, GNR and LNWR. The situation during this period became a complex one. In brief, events developed as follows.

It was mentioned previously that the LNWR and MR companies had been planning an amalgamation.

In 1854 the Government, in the interests of trying to provide the country with a satisfactory railway system, came down against large railway monopolies and at the same time indicated that it wished to see co-operation between different companies in the exchange of traffic and various facilities at the point of junction. As a result of this, by March 1854, the LNWR and MR dropped their scheme for a possible amalgamation. This brought relief in NWR circles for any such amalgamation would have ruled out the need for a route to Scotland over their metals and hence the need for the Orton Branch, at least as far as the LNWR and MR companies were concerned. However, these two companies, having ostensibly broken off the proposed merger, entered, quite illegally, into a 'common purse' arrangement. This agreement became, in effect, public knowledge a few years after but in the meantime these two companies worked together in this way with MR trains running into London from the Midlands and Yorkshire by joining the LNWR line at Rugby. The 'common purse' agreement was to the detriment of the GNR, also working from the same areas into London, and was calculated to be so. It was felt, no doubt, by the LNWR and MR, that having reached Leeds from London, the GNR's advancement must be checked by attempting to reduce the latter's traffic receipts.

As a result of the arrangement between the LNWR and the MR, the latter had little time for the demands and well-being of the NWR. This not only resulted in the Orton Branch northwards beyond Ingleton remaining unfinished but also of without any prospect of being completed. Again the NWR considered going back to the GNR for support because, by the end of 1854, the extension of time granted by Parliament for the completion of the branch was rapidly running out, diminishing any hope of building the line within the time allotted. So the NWR decided to try the MR again and no doubt seeing the possible potential danger of GNR action, the MR did, for a time consider co-operating with the L&C in order to complete the branch. Yet again the outcome was as it had been before, namely that the MR and L&C could not come to an agreement. The NWR now turned to the GNR once again and company showed some interest, being prepared to consider the Orton Branch as part of a route to Scotland. It also considered applying to Parliament for running powers over the MR from Leeds to Skipton in order to make the whole scheme feasible. On the brink of a decision, in December, the GNR was approached by the LNWR. This company, even with the state of enmity which existed between it and the GNR, was prepared to sink some of its pride to prevent the latter going north independently or using the NWR.

After discussion, the GNR was invited to join the arrangement for pooling traffic and for the moment it found this a more agreeable idea than attempting to build the Orton Branch. The result, again, was that a scheme to build this branch had been foiled. By now the NWR really felt the pressures of the companies around it could be tolerated no longer. The climax came early in 1855 after the L&C had a minor dispute with the LNWR. Seizing the opportunity, the NWR moved in to try and take advantage of the situation and suggested that it and the L&C should weaken the power of the LNWR by constructing the Orton Branch between them. But despite the differences, the LNWR had considerable power on the L&C Board and, as a result, the NWR plan was turned down.

This seemed to be the last straw as far as the NWR was concerned and so, in a desperate bid, it decided to go it alone. The Directors knew the company could not afford to build the Orton Branch and as the time extension was almost exhausted a new Bill would be needed. A decision was made the revise the plans somewhat and in 1855 the company prepared to present a Bill before Parliament which would have a considerable impact on the other companies. Indeed, they were to be rocked back on their heels by what followed. All, that is, except the GNR: it began to see the hope of a route to Scotland materializing at last.

Chapter Two

Rival Schemes
1855 to 1857

1855

The scheme drawn up by the NWR in 1855, ready for the Parliamentary Session of 1856, was a most ambitious one, although the actual proposals for the Orton Branch were not very far reaching. The plan involved a deviation for the original line, whereby there would be no junction with the L&C at Dillicar but the line would continue up the eastern side of the Lune Valley, crossing the River Lune and joining the L&C main line just south of Tebay. This change, in itself, was not felt to have any great significance, although, if approved, it did raise the question of whether, at a later date, the NWR might take a branch from this to join one of the lines coming into Tebay from north-eastern England. The extension, however, did not mean a saving which would enable the NWR to build the branch and therefore, from that point of view, would not have meant an earlier completion of the line.

In other clauses of the Bill the NWR did make some startling demands. The one which was potentially the most damaging was in Clause 4. This included an application for extensive running powers over the lines of other companies, including the GNR, MR, L&C, CR and the Glasgow and South Western Railway. Here, truly, was a thrust for a shorter route to Scotland. Also included in Clause 5 of the Bill was an application for permission for the NWR to lease or sell its undertaking to the MR, the L&C or the GNR. This sale would include the powers in the Bill as a whole. Perhaps, needless to say, the Bill met with considerable opposition.

It was mentioned previously that the LNWR had been working a common purse agreement with the MR and Midland traffic for London used its ally's line south of Rugby. The proposed new route to Scotland was in the interests of neither of these companies. Also opposed to the scheme were the Lancashire and Yorkshire Railway and the North Eastern Railway, the former having interests in the North-West and the latter hoping that a route to Scotland would come its way through eastern England. The wrath of the L&C was probably the greatest and spurred this company to do more than simply oppose the Bill in 1856.

The ally of the NWR was now the GNR, although this company did have misgivings about the application in the Bill for extensive running

LANCASTER AND CARLISLE AND INGLETON RAILWAY

(Construction of Railway from the Lancaster and Carlisle Railway to the North Western Railway, at or near Ingleton, with Branch; Incorporation of New Company; Powers of Construction and Subscription to Lancaster and Carlisle and North Western Railway Companies, and Transfer of Powers; Amendment of Acts).

NOTICE IS HEREBY GIVEN, That application is intended to be made to Parliament in the next Session for an Act to make and maintain a Railway, with all proper works, stations, and conveniences connected therewith, to commence by a junction with the Lancaster and Carlisle Railway, at or near Scufton House, in the township of Dillicar, in the parish of Kendal, otherwise Kirkby Kendal, otherwise Kirkby in Kendal, in the county of Westmoreland, thence to pass from, through, or into the several parishes, townships, extra-parochial, or other places following, or some of them (videlicet), Orton, Tebay, Dillicar Smithy, Dillicar, Docker, Low Gill, Grayrigg, Lambrigg, Kendal, Kirkby Kendal, Kirkby in Kendal, Kirkland, Firbank, Firbank High, Firbank Low, Killington, Middleton, Raisemoor, Mansergh, Barbon, Beckford, Beckford, Beckfoot. Barbon Beckfoot, Low Casterton, High Casterton, Casterton, Kirkby Lonsdale, Whinfell, Deans Biggin, Burrow with Burrow, Overborough, Overtown, Burrow, High Burrow, Low Burrow, Over Burrow, Leck, High Leck, Low Leck, Tunstall, all in the county of Westmoreland; Sedbergh, Howgill, Bland, Upper Bland, Nether Bland, Briggfiat, Cautley, and Dowbiggin, Howgill with Bland, Marthwaite, Dent, Ewcross, Newby, Newby Coate, Thornton, Thornton in Lonsdale, Westhouse, High Westhouse, Low Westhouse, Westhouses, Burton, Burton in Lonsdale, Black Burton, Masongill, Bentham, Coldcotes, Coldcoates, Moorgarth, Twistleton, and Ingleton, all in the West Riding of the county of York; and Ireby, Ireby with Tatham, Tatham with Ireby, Cowen Bridge, Thornton in Lonsdale, Tunstall, Cantsfield, Leck, High Leck, Low Leck, Burrow, Burrow with Burrow, High Burrow, Low Burrow, Over Burrow, Overtown, Overborough, and Whittington, all in the county palatine of Lancaster; and to terminate by a junction with the northerly Branch or Line of the North Western Railway, at or near the station thereof at Ingleton, in the township of Ingleton, in the parish of Bentham, in the West Riding of the county of York, and also a Railway, with all proper works, stations, and conveniences connected therewith, diverging from the said intended new Railway at or near Day-bank, otherwise Davy-bank Farm, in the township of Firbank and parish of Kirkby Lonsdale, passing from, through, or into the several parishes, townships, extra-parochial and other places following, or some of them; (that is to say,) Kirkby Lonsdale, Firbank, Firbank High, Firbank Low, Kirkland, Kendal, Kirkby Kendal, Kirkby in Kendal, Lambrigg.

Reproduction of the Lancaster and Carlisle and Ingleton Railway Bill of 1856.
Author's Collection

Greyrigg, Docker, Dillicar, and Dillicar Smithy, all in the county of Westmoreland, and terminating by a junction with the Lancaster and Carlisle Railway, near the quarter mile-post indicating twenty-seven and a quarter miles from the junction of the Lancaster and Carlisle with the Lancaster and Preston Junction Railway near Lancaster :

And it is also intended by such Act to take power to stop up, alter, or divert, whether temporarily or permanently, all turnpike and other roads and highways, railways, tramways, aqueducts, canals, streams, rivers, sewers, mains, and pipes, which it may be necessary to stop up, alter, or divert, for the purpose of the construction of the said intended Railway, Branch Railway, and works, or any of them :

And to take powers for purchasing or taking lands and buildings by compulsion or agreement for the purposes of the said undertaking, and for levying tolls, rates, and duties in respect thereof, and to grant exemptions from tolls, rates, and duties :

And the said Bill will either incorporate a Company for the purpose of carrying the said intended undertaking, or some part thereof, into effect, or will authorise the Lancaster and Carlisle Railway Company and the North Western Railway Company, or either of them, and either jointly or separately, to execute the said works, and to carry the purposes of the said Act into execution, and to apply their respective corporate funds to all or any of the purposes aforesaid, or to raise additional capital for the same purposes, by borrowing on mortgage or bond, or by the creation of new shares in their respective undertakings, either with or without preference or priority in payment of interest or dividend, or with or without other special rights and privileges :

And in the event of a Company being incorporated for the purposes of the said Act, or of the Lancaster and Carlisle Railway Company being empowered to carry the same into effect, the said Act will provide that such new Company, or the Lancaster and Carlisle Railway Company, as the case may be, may delegate and transfer to the North Western Railway Company all or any of the powers of the said intended Act; and in such event the said Bill will authorise that Company to apply their corporate funds to the construction and maintenance of the said Railway, Branch Railway, and works, or any of them, or to take shares in and to subscribe for or towards the said undertaking, or to guarantee such interest or profit upon the outlay or any part thereof as may be agreed upon, and to raise money for the several purposes aforesaid or any of them, and to increase their capital by the creation of new shares, either with or without preference or priority in payment of interest or dividend, or with or without other special rights or privileges, or by mortgage, or by such other ways or means as Parliament shall think fit :

And the said intended Act will also provide for the alteration or amendment of "The Lancaster and Preston Junction Railway Amendment Act, 1849," and for fixing and ascertaining and (if need be) altering the rights, privileges, obligations, and liabilities of the Lancaster and Preston Junction and Lancaster and Carlisle Railway Companies respectively under that Act, in relation to the said intended undertaking, and the share and interest therein which may belong to or be assumed by the Lancaster and Carlisle Railway Company under the provisions of the said intended Act, or in such other manner and for such other purposes as may be agreed upon by and between the said last-mentioned Companies :

3

And for carrying into effect all or any of the above objects, and so far as may be necessary for such purposes, but not further or otherwise, it is intended by the said Act to alter, extend, amend, and enlarge, and, if need be, to repeal all or any of the powers and provisions of the several Acts relating to the Lancaster and Carlisle and North Western Railway Companies respectively:

And Notice is hereby further given, That a published map, and plans, and sections, describing the lines and levels of the said intended Railway and Branch Railway, and the lands proposed to be taken for the purposes thereof, together with a book of reference to such plans, and a copy of this Notice, as published in the London Gazette, will be deposited before the 30th day of November, 1856, with the clerk of the peace for the county of Westmoreland, at his office in Appleby; with the clerk of the peace for the West Riding of the county of York, at his office in Wakefield; and with the clerk of the peace for the county of Lancaster, at his office in Preston; and that copies of so much of the said several plans, sections, and books of reference as relate to the several parishes and extra-parochial places in or through which the said intended Railway and Branch Railway are proposed to be made, together with a copy of this Notice, as published in the London Gazette, will be deposited before the said 30th day of November, as follows, viz.: in the case of parishes, with the clerks of such parishes respectively, at their respective places of abode; and in the case of any extra-parochial place, with the clerk of some parish immediately adjoining such extra-parochial place:

And Notice is hereby further given, That printed copies of the proposed Bill will be deposited in the Private Bill Office of the House of Commons on or before the 31st day of December, in the present year.

Dated this 12th day of November, 1856.

SWIFT AND WAGSTAFF,

32, *Great George Street,*

Westminster.

powers. The GNR had eventually gone against the pooling arrangement with the LNWR and the result had been a stiff rate war in which the GNR came off very badly. Now the GNR saw something of a way out and a solution to its problem.

The NWR Bill was attacked from the very outset by the L&C because it saw that apart from other matters, there was a flagrant violation in the NWR Acts of 1846 and 1852 regarding the sale or lease of the section of line from Up Hall to Dillicar. The L&C tried to stop the Bill ever being presented by taking proceedings in the Court of Chancery, but failed. After a very rough passage, the Bill was read for a second time. The proposed deviation to Tebay was not approved but the NWR Directors probably lost no sleep over that. The main thing was that the Commons Committee decided that the NWR route over the Orton Branch was the shortest route to Scotland and was therefore desirable.

Then came a major setback for the NWR. The companies opposing the Bill attacked the real core of it when it came up for the Third Reading, namely the application for running powers. Here the NWR lost the fight. Whilst the route via the Orton Branch was desirable, the Commons, in accordance with the policies laid down in 1854, did not feel that the powers the NWR were seeking were necessary to achieve the route and so application for running powers was turned down. At this the NWR withdrew the Bill. For the moment it decided to think again.

One effect of the whole proceedings surrounding the Bill was to bring to light the fact that a 'common purse' was being worked by the LNWR and MR. Although this was initially denied by the two companies, it was later admitted and the practice terminated. The MR, thus split from the LNWR, gradually leaned towards the GNR for a time. A line from Leicester to join the latter at Hitchin was almost complete and this was to give the MR a route into the capital at Kings Cross. Soon the MR and LNWR were to be at variance over the Orton Branch, as were, for that matter, the MR and GNR over the use of Kings Cross.

The L&C spent £3,000 opposing the NWR Bill but no doubt felt the expense justified. In the aftermath, the NWR did not seem daunted. It had withdrawn its Bill but simply to reassess the situation and prepare for another attempt in the Parliamentary Session of 1857.

For the L&C the whole business had been too close for comfort. The Directors decided on positive action. If the Orton Branch was to be built, and it seemed that it would be, then their company had better be the one to do the building. As a result the company had the route surveyed and plans drawn up.

1857

The Lancaster and Carlisle steps in

On 13th January 1857, a special meeting of the shareholders of the L & C was called and held at the Castle Station, Lancaster. This was to inform them of the situation and to ask them for their support. Before the meeting a circular had been issued for the benefit of the shareholders and this set out a summary of the events leading up to the Directors' decision.

The Directors stressed the point that the NWR seemed unable to construct the branch. They also reminded members of the attempts by that company to break off earlier agreements and, further, what was seen as a most important matter, the fact that the NWR intended to introduce another Bill into Parliament in that year which was similar to the one that had been put forward the previous year. The Directors took the view that the branch must be constructed for the benefit of the country as well as their company. It was pointed out that the profits from the branch would probably not be very large. Further, the Directors emphasized in the circular that it was not and never would be the policy of the L&C to build branch lines because these could well involve the company in unjustifiable expenses. However, here, they maintained, was an exception.

In short, what the Directors were probably getting at was that the Government had approved the Ingleton route as the shortest route to Scotland and so the line would almost certainly be built by one company or another. In these circumstances it was clearly desirable that the L&C should be the one to do the building. In addition, in this way the threats of the NWR would be removed once and for all together with the possibility of another company encroaching on the L&C territory in the event of the forthcoming Bill of the NWR being successful.

The cost of the line was estimated at £300,000 and at the special meeting at least one shareholder suggested that it might be worth risking another £3,000 fighting the NWR Bill rather than committing to spend £300,000 in building a new line! However, it was generally agreed that the NWR might be successful and somehow construct the line. It was also realized only too well that the GNR supported the NWR in the scheme and with this in mind some of the shareholders expressed concern that the former might construct the line or provide the capital for it.

The outcome of the meeting was a unanimous decision to support the Directors in their plan to present a Bill to Parliament seeking permission to build the line. By the first half-yearly meeting of the L&C in March

1857 it was possible to report that the Bill had been read for a second time in Parliament.

The Two Schemes

Considered side by side, the two schemes before Parliament, that of the L&C and also the NWR, did not differ greatly. The countryside of the Yorkshire Dales does not allow a great choice of routes if costs were to be kept down and the expenses of earthworks and building bridges minimized.

From Ingleton the plans of both companies showed similar routes. In fact, as mentioned earlier, the NWR already held a number of fields as far as Cowan Bridge. This company now intended to use these whilst the L&C hoped to purchase them.

Both projected lines passed within about a mile of Kirkby Lonsdale and then turned northwards into the Lune Valley which, at this point, is quite wide and fairly flat. Along this valley both proposed routes passed through Casterton, Barbon and Middleton but after Middleton the schemes differ. The route proposed by the NWR continued directly northwards whilst that of the L&C made a one mile semi-circular deviation eastwards to approach the market town of Sedbergh. This difference is perhaps significant. The NWR saw the line as being part of a direct trunk route to Scotland and was not therefore prepared to make a considerable detour for a small township (compare the Bills for 1848 and 1852). The L&C, on the other hand, seemed to have plans which gave some priority to local traffic.

After this difference in the plans, the two lines come together near the River Lune, to the north-west of Sedbergh, but then diverge again. At this point the Lune Valley becomes much narrower and has steep sides. The proposed L&C line would pass up the west side of the valley to Lowgill, whereas the NWR line would hold to the east side and along the Lune Gorge almost to Tebay. The 1856 proposals of the NWR, for the line north of Lowgill, were modified slightly from those of those in 1855. In the former, the line would have followed a path much closer to the Lune and crossed the river twice, in addition to the final crossing south of Tebay, as in the 1855 plans (*see map page 6*).

One further point about the L&C scheme. The plans included a short spur from the branch to the main line south of Lowgill so providing facilities for southbound connections. As planned it would only have been a mile long and therefore short enough for the overall junction at

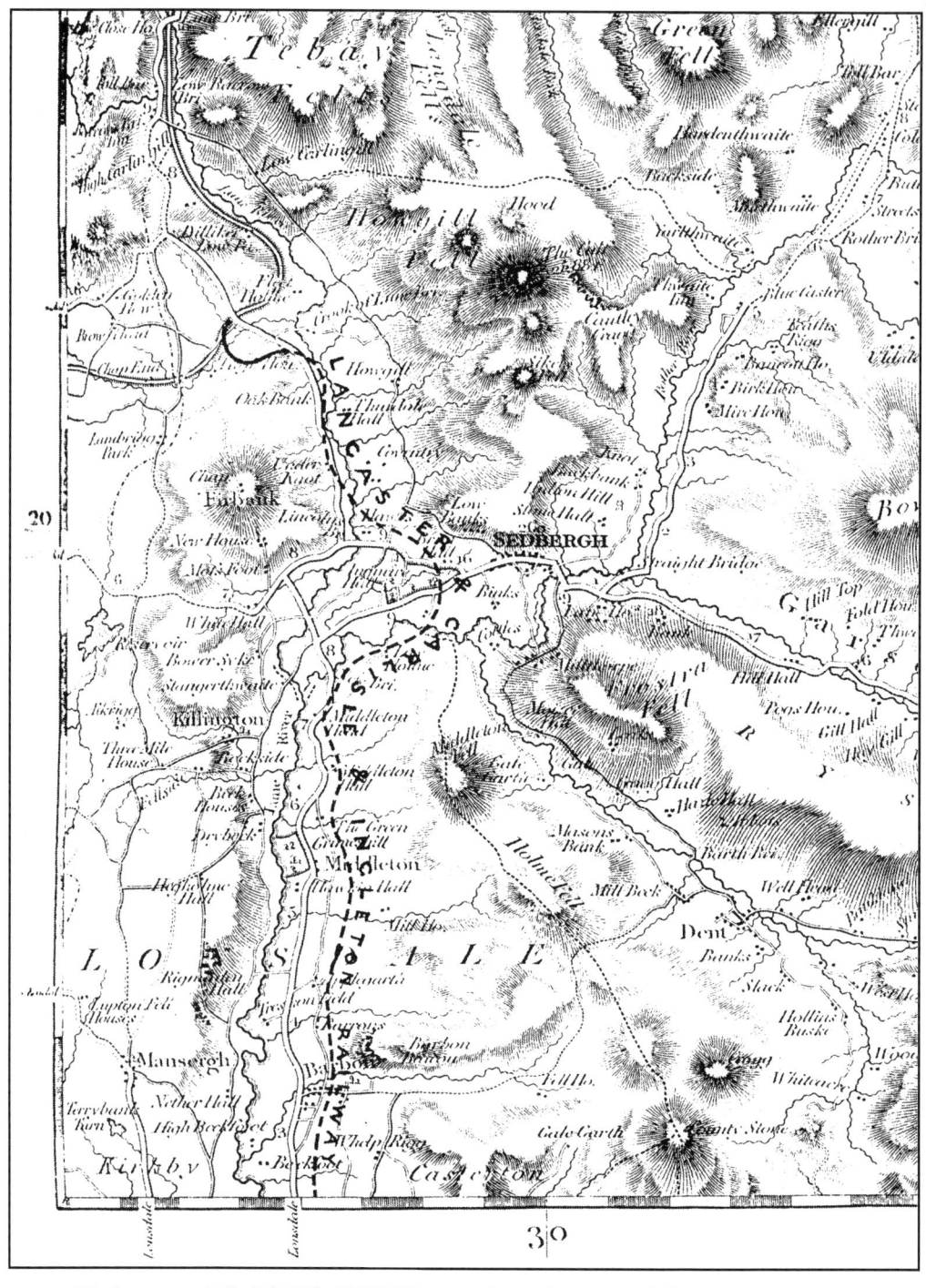

The Lancaster & Carlisle Bill of 1857. This map shows the proposed sharp curve at Lowgill (black unbroken line – but red on the original) which had to be modified.

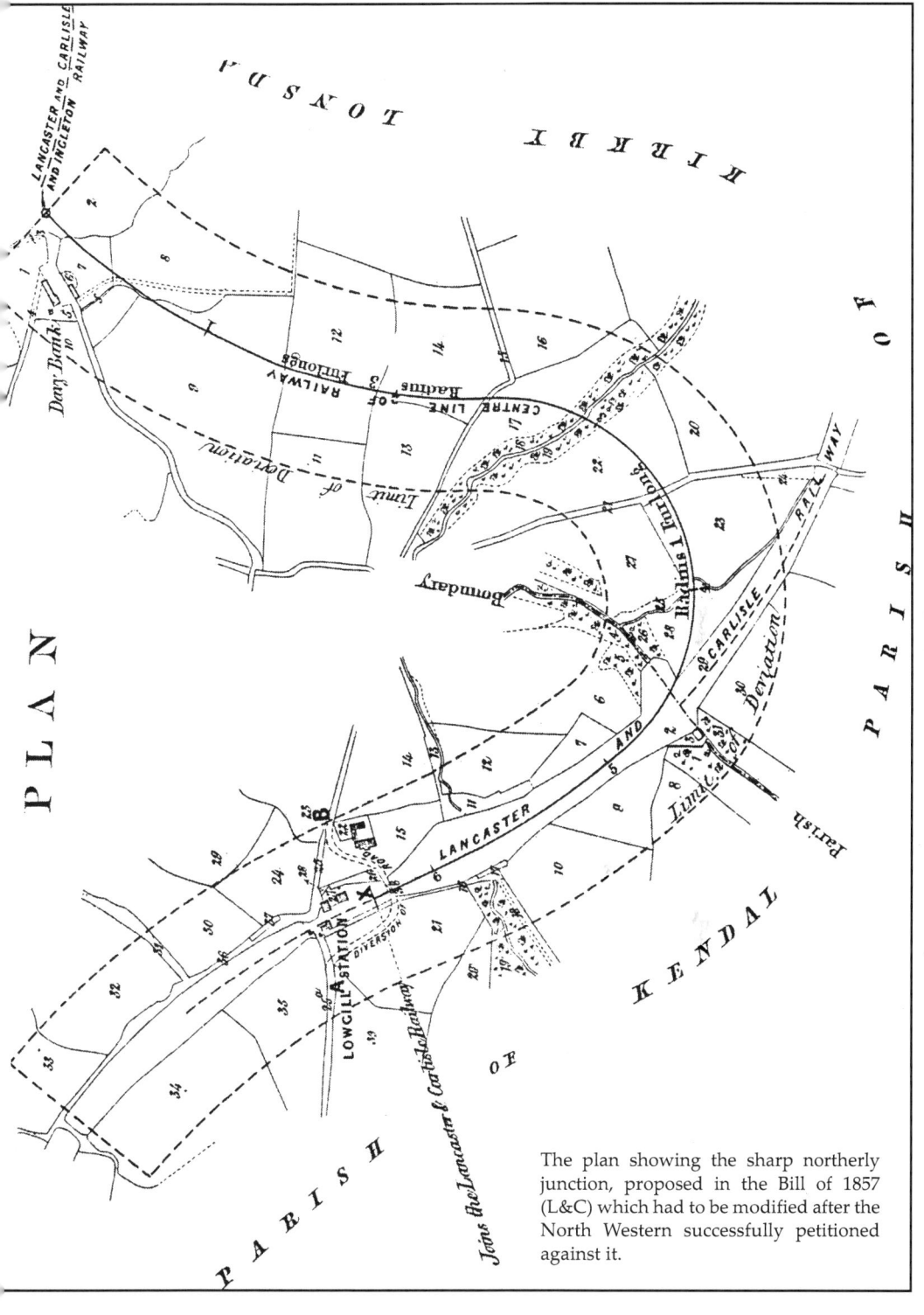

The plan showing the sharp northerly junction, proposed in the Bill of 1857 (L&C) which had to be modified after the North Western successfully petitioned against it.

Lowgill to be described as a forked one.

Although the cost of the proposed NWR scheme was lower than that of its original scheme, the route in effect duplicated a stretch of the L&C main line (opened in 1846) north of Lowgill and this stretch, in very difficult terrain through the Lune Gorge.

The Commons Committee decides

In June the findings of the Commons Committee were made known. The L&C proposals had been accepted as the better scheme. At the same time the NWR received Parliamentary sanction to abandon its scheme and the L&C was given leave to purchase the various plots of land already purchased for use on the route. It also received permission to purchase the foundation works of the Ingleton viaduct.

The Parliamentary Committee made it quite clear that in granting the L&C the authority to construct the line, it considered that its use was to be seen essentially as part of a through route 'From Carlisle to the southern, midland and eastern part of England'.

After participating in the Parliamentary proceedings, the MR and the GNR withdrew to view the result with satisfaction. The Directors of the GNR, reporting in August, welcomed 'the prospect of the gap of twenty-three miles between Ingleton and Tebay being filled up, whereby the company [GNR] will become, with the Midland, the Lancaster and Carlisle and the Caledonian, the shortest route to Scotland'. They added, 'The expense of the line in question has been thrown upon the Lancaster and Carlisle Company who are better able to afford it than the North Western'.

It was indeed very satisfactory for the GNR because after all the negotiating of the previous years, it seemed that it was soon to achieve its ambition of a route to Scotland without having to contribute to the cost of constructing the Orton Branch. The MR, too, depending now on the GNR for access to a London terminal also felt that the business had been concluded in a satisfactory manner.

So, the feeling was one of optimism but this optimism was to be short lived because the MR and GNR were not to have a long lasting alliance. Nevertheless, for the moment, all seemed well.

J.E.Errington, the L&C Engineer, who, incidentally, became the Vice-President of the Institution of Civil Engineers in 1861 but died in 1862, went ahead with his plans. The name 'Orton Branch' was dropped in favour of 'The Lune Valley Line', possibly symbolic of a clean sweep and a new start. For a time the L&C styled itself 'The Lancaster and Carlisle and Ingleton Railway' as if to drive the point home. However, it soon reassumed its original title.

1858

One or two elements in the plans were changed in the early stages.

The junction with the main line at Lowgill became a matter of dispute. At the half-yearly meeting of the shareholders in March, the members were made aware that a Bill was going forward to modify the northerly section and this included the removal of the short branch which would facilitate a southbound connection. J.J. Wilson was keen to point out that during the proceedings to gain Parliamentary approval to build the line, great emphasis had been laid on the importance and advantage of a forked junction, yet it now seemed, without good reason, to be of no importance. He was strongly supported in this view by G.L. Braithwaite but Hassel pointed out that the saving on expenses in removing this short branch would be considerable and the Engineer had seen fit to change the plan.

An Objection by the NWR

There was also an objection when the Bill came up for consideration in the Parliamentary proceedings. The NWR raised an issue about the curvature of the line at the junction with the main line. The curve on the plans showed a section that would be very sharp and would result in fast traffic having to slow down when about the join the main line. The NWR was successful in this petition and the L&C was obliged to modify the severity of the curve. The outcome was that the line could not follow the line of the valley side before joining the main line and this necessitated the building of a large viaduct, a structure which was to become a landmark for many miles.

The position of Lowgill station had to be changed because the existing station was too far south to serve both main line and branch. In spite of this its relocation was still to the south of the junction and so the main line and branch had to have separate platforms.

With the plans finalized and Parliamentary matters settled, J.E. Errington was ready for work to begin. The time for completion, as laid down by Parliament, was four years and with this in view, arrangements were made to invite tenders for the work on various sections of the branch.

206.—LANCASTER AND CARLISLE.

(LEASED TO LONDON AND NORTH WESTERN).

Incorporated by 7 and 8 Vic., cap. 37 (1844), for a single line in the first instance until the act authorising the Caledonian was passed, when it was made a double line, continuing the Lancaster and Preston to Carlisle, and there forming a junction with the Caledonian. Length, 70 miles.

An act, 23 Vic., cap. 87 (1st August, 1849), sanctioned an agreement between this company and the Lancaster and Preston, as follows:—That the Lancaster and Preston receives 7-22nds and the Lancaster and Carlisle the remaining 15-22nds of net profits derived from working of both lines. Out of their proportion the Lancaster and Preston paid interest on mortgage debt, 113,000*l*.

By 20 and 21 Vic., cap. 151 (25th August, 1857), the Lancaster and Carlisle was authorised to construct the connecting link between Tebay and Ingleton. Additional capital, 300,000*l*.; loan, 100,000*l*. Length of main line is 19 miles; that of the branch, 1 mile 2 furlongs 1 chain. By 21 and 22 Vic. (23rd July, 1858), the company obtained power to abandon part of Lowgill Junction, the connection between Little North Western and Lancaster and Carlise being in no degree impaired. Opened October 1st, 1861.

By 22 and 23 Vic., cap. 124 (August 13th, 1859), the acts of the company were consolidated, and lease and amalgamation with the Kendal and Windermere and Lancaster and Preston authorised.

DIRECTORS:

Chairman—E. W. HASELL, Esq., Dalemain, Penrith.
Deputy-Chairman—WILLIAM JACKSON, Esq., Lancaster.

Samuel Edward Bolden, Esq., Newbold Comyn, Leamington.
Edward Hughes Satterthwaite, Esq., Lancaster.
George H. Head, Esq., Rickerby House, Carlisle.
John Coulston, Esq., Hawkshead, Lancaster.
William Birley, Esq., Preston.
†Hon. Col. Lowther, M.P., Barley Thorpe, Oakham, Rutlandshire.
‡John T. Hibbert, Esq., M.P., Urmston Grange, Stretford, near Manchester.
‡George Hall Lawrence, Esq., Mossley Hill, Liverpool.
William Nicholson Hodgson, Esq., M.P., Newby Grange, Carlisle.
‡James Bancroft, Esq., Manchester.
‡Alexander Brogden, Esq., Ulverston.
‡James Cropper, Esq., Ellergreen, Kendal.
Henry Garnett, Esq., Wyreside, near Lancaster.
W. A. F. Saunders, Esq., Wennington Hall, Lancaster.
John Barker, Esq., of Broughton Lodge, Newton-in-Cartmel.

† Nominated by the Earl of Lonsdale. ‡ L. and N. W.

OFFICERS.—Sec., William King; Auditors, Joseph Salkeld and Henry Crosfield; Bankers, The Lancaster Banking Company, Lancaster.

Head Offices—Lancaster.

Extract from the 1866 *Bradshaw's Railway Manual*.

Chapter Three

Construction
1858 to 1861

1858
The contracts

The scheme drawn up for the purpose of constructing the Lune Valley Line split it into three contracts but it was decided, after considering the fact that a large viaduct would have to be built at the northern end, to subdivide one of these which in effect made four.

The first contract was for a section from Lowgill for a distance of five miles and forty-four chains but this was subsequently divided into Contract 1 and Contract 1A.

Contract 1A

This was for a distance of one mile and six chains from Lowgill and the main work in it was the Lowgill viaduct. This viaduct would have 11 arches each of 45 feet span and stride the valley of the Dillicar Beck. It would be built of Penrith stone and be 90 feet above the valley floor at one point.

Contract 1

This covered the next four miles and thirty-eight chains, stretching as far south as the bridge spanning the River Rawthey, near Sedbergh, and including the bridge. This contract, dealing with the section of the Lune Valley which is narrow and steep, included a considerable amount of earthwork. There would be two significant bridges in this section; one over the River Lune, also to be built of Penrith sandstone, which would be 530 feet long and 100 feet high and the one over the River Rawthey. The Rawthey bridge would have a span of 120 feet and be built at an angle of 38° to the line of the railway. Both bridges would have a centre metal arch, cast in the same way.

Contract 2

This consisted of the next seven miles and twenty-seven chains. This section would pass through part of the Lune Valley where the terrain is much flatter and so, it was anticipated, present no major problem.

Contract 3

The rest of the line down to Ingleton formed this section, a distance of five miles and seventy-eight chains. The major work on this contract would be the Ingleton viaduct which would have 11 arches, each with a 57 feet span, have a length of 800 feet and be 80 feet above the River Greta. It would be built in white sandstone taken from a quarry near

Bentham. There would also to be a small viaduct at Leck consisting of five arches. The line would be double track.

Contract 1 was, without doubt, the most demanding and so tenders were invited for this section first. Notices were put out on 27th February. The sealed tenders were to be delivered no later than 19th April.

At the half-yearly meeting on 5th March, the Directors announced that all the rails needed for the line had been purchased. Land purchases were also made. These generally consisted of small parcels of ground but one piece deserves a mention. From the Lune crossing to Middleton, the line would pass through the lands of the Ingmire Estate, with the exception of a small stretch of common land at the bottom of Holme Fell, near Sedbergh. This substantial portion of Ingmire Estate, the largest single plot by far, cost the L&C £7,395 15s. 0d. and was purchased from Eliza Upton.

By the summer all was ready for the construction work on Contract 1 to begin. The successful tender was made by Coulthard and Allen and so they would return to the branch after having left it 10 years before, when working for the NWR.

The first sod was cut by W.A.Saunders, of Wennington Hall. He was an eminent director of the L&C.

In September, at the half-yearly meeting, Errington was able to inform the members that work was progressing favourably and that he was soon to invite tenders for the rest of the line.

Advertisements were put out on 18th September for Contracts 2 and 3 and tenders had to be in by 11th October. Subsequently, these tenders were awarded to James Taylor and work on these sections had begun by the end of the year.

All seemed to be going well and events were only marred by some accidents. In the initial stages these were relatively minor and involved falls of earth. Haworth Matteson sustained a broken leg on 16th August and Joseph Airey a similar mishap on 21st September. However, on the 3rd November, the first fatal accident occurred on the works. It happened at Firbank, on Contract 1, in a cutting to the west of what was then the turnpike road leading to Lowgill. The men had just started work, early in the morning, on a section which had been sub-contracted to Robert Swindlehurst. There was a sudden fall of earth some 10 yards in length and one man, Roger Parker, of Sedbergh, was completely buried. Thomas Banks had both legs broken and a third man received minor injuries. The two injured men were removed to a group of huts near the works of the Lune viaduct which, by then, was under construction.

1859

By January, the plans for the northerly junction of the line had been fully settled with the decision taken to build a large viaduct at Lowgill. This work had been advertised as Contract 1A and was awarded to Samuel Buxton of Leeds.

On 4th January at a special ceremony, W.A.Saunders laid the foundation stone of this major work. Mr Buxton presented Mr Saunders with a silver trowel inscribed with the words 'Presented to W.A.F.Saunders Esq. of Wennington Hall by Samuel Buxton of Leeds, contractor, on the laying of the first stone of the Dillicar Viaduct. 5th January 1859'.

J.E.Errington made a short speech in which he emphasized the magnitude of the work which would include almost 400,000 cubic feet of masonry.

There followed a speech made by the Chairman of the company, E.W. Hassel. He congratulated himself and his fellow Directors on having chosen Samuel Buxton to undertake the work, for 'he is a man renowned for his energy and perseverance'. The Chairman also took the opportunity to refer to the provision of a reading room where papers and periodicals would be provided. This room was also to be a place where a lecture would be given on each Sabbath. Mr James Cropper welcomed the provision of the reading and lecture room and stated his willingness to provide papers and a minister for Sunday instruction. The foreman carpenter replied on behalf of the men and this was followed by three rousing cheers. In accordance with the usual practice on such an occasion, the men were provided with a meal on the site whilst the Directors went off to celebrate at The Black Bull in Sedbergh.

The day, unfortunately, ended in tragedy. Three men, returning home after the celebrations at Lowgill, decided to walk back along the main line and were run down by a Carlisle-bound express. Two received fatal injuries.

Samuel Buxton's much praised energy and perseverance were very much taxed by a wet spring. The work was delayed by inclement weather, characteristic of the area, and fell behind schedule. The weather also resulted in considerable changes in the workforce and it is reported that many men only stayed a few weeks. They were discouraged by the inclement weather and also the lack of any suitable amenities in the locality for spending what little leisure time they had. Throughout the whole construction period, labour was hard to find.

On 4th March, at the first half-yearly meeting of the shareholders,

Errington made his report on the progress and stated that work on the viaduct at Lowgill was not progressing as planned. He did add that the work had been reorganized somewhat and laid out in a manner which he hoped would assist in enabling progress to be more rapid. He commented, too, on the slow progress in general, pointing out that the wet season had resulted in soft ground and the subsequent difficulty in getting a solid foundation down. A committee was set up to advise on the project and this included Messrs Saunders, Cropper and Hassel. The object was to look at how progress might be speeded up.

On the same day as the half-yearly meeting, work was started on the Ingleton viaduct. Here there was no ceremony, the foundations having already been laid by the NWR Company. Forty men were employed to complete this other fine viaduct which the line would boast.

The work continued to progress steadily elsewhere but there were more fatal accidents.

On 30th March an elderly man named Waller was buried under a fall of earth near Borrett Hill, near Sedbergh and his body was badly mutilated. On 1st July, William Taylforth was killed whilst working a crane at the viaduct being built over the River Lune. It seems that he put it into gear instead of putting the brake on and as a result was struck by some part of the mechanism. On 27th August, Thomas Walpole was killed in a cutting near Dillicar by yet another fall of earth.

In spite of these unfortunate events, work went on apace. The Lune Valley echoed to the sound of railway construction work and the local people, it is said, 'watched in awe 'as the line took shape.

No doubt many, by now, living in the locality may have had some experience of what a railway was like because not so very far away, 'over the hill', towards Kendal it was a common sight with the L&C main line in operation and the line to Kendal open as well. Even so, not all would get this far and no doubt there was probably excitement in some quarters that a railway line would soon be close at hand.

One observer left a vivid first-hand account of the prevailing operation. Julia Green Vigour, daughter of the Reverend Isaac Green, the perpetual curate of Howgill at the time, wrote the following in her book entitled *Recollections of Sedbergh School and Town in Early Victorian Days*.

She wrote:

Far in the fifties was begun the Branch Railway between Lowgill and Ingleton:

the whole town and countryside swarmed with navvies, a very fine set of men physically, and always to us exceedingly nice, though free of speech and personal comments. They simply filled Sedbergh cottages to overflowing, besides the rows and rows of turf huts near the railway works. Previously the nearest main line station was Lowgill, five miles distant and people got there as best they could: a carrier's cart conveyed all the baggage of the scholar lads at Christmas and Midsummer. The coming of the Branch Railway in 1857 brought many changes. We got used to the navvies; they made a change in the old-time life of our town which lasted on. We watched the railway grow and the bridges built, Jackdaw and Lune viaducts and felt sad over the accidents, about one fatal accident for every mile of the railway, especially sad if we had known the man by sight. Most accidents occurred at the Lune Viaduct. The Lowgill Viaduct was too far for ordinary walks but we sometimes drove there. Business looked up in Sedbergh and has seemed to prosper, especially in the food shops, ever since.

Clearly Julia Green Vigour enjoyed her trips to watch the works in progress!

The LNWR seeks to lease the L & C

In September, the second half-yearly meeting of the shareholders was held. Before a report was given on the progress of 'The Lune Valley Line' it was announced that the L&C had been approached by the LNWR. The LNWR had made an offer for the lease of the L&C line; this to be in perpetuity.

Involved in this were the last moves for the control of the line from Ingleton to Lowgill and the LNWR was eventually to gain this control when the shareholders agreed to the terms.

At this meeting, Errington also gave his report. This time it was a more favourable one because more progress had been made possible during the summer months. Contract 1A had a quarter of the earthworks completed and the Lowgill viaduct was well advanced. Contract 1 was also inside schedule and in parts even the boundary fencing for the line was in place. More than half of the earthworks were completed and 21 out of 27 culverts finished, together with 10 of the 17 bridges. The viaduct over the Lune, often, by this stage, being referred to as the Waterside Viaduct, had, by this time, three of the six arches almost turned and the other piers and abutments were nearly at springing level. At the Rawthey viaduct, also now locally being referred to as 'Jackdaw viaduct' because of the numerous quantities of these birds nesting in the vicinity, the north abutment was above the water level and the other not far behind. In addition about a mile of track had been laid and another ballasted in readiness.

Further south on Contracts 2 and 3, the work was not as far advanced but, as Errington pointed out, these sections had been started later. The ground of Contract 2 had been broken in seven places and the two heaviest road approaches were well advanced. Eight of the culverts were complete together with a quarter of the fencing and one-fifth of the earthworks. Difficulty had been encountered at Casterton where rock had to be blasted to make a cutting but the problem had been resolved.

On Contract 3, more than one-third of the earthworks had been completed and 14 of the 24 bridges had been either constructed or were already in the course of being so. Construction had already started on the small five-arch viaduct at Leck, near Cowan Bridge, and at Ingleton two of the 11 arches of the viaduct were almost complete and six others had piers which were well advanced.

Errington was satisfied. He was quite convinced that the whole work would be completed well within the stipulated period of four years. He also pointed out that detailed plans for the station sidings and approaches were well in hand as were the materials which would be needed.

Later in the year, during September, there was a meeting of The Lunesdale Agricultural Association at Kirkby Lonsdale. Local feeling among farmers about the coming of the railway was reflected in some of the chairman's remarks. He commented that he was glad to hear that a railway was coming into their immediate vicinity, bringing with it the facilities for the conveyance to fresh markets in order to take the farm produce out of their hands. He added 'Where fresh lines spring into existence there would be found fresh markets also (Cheers!) It was a well-known fact that railways had done this good – that they had the effect of equalizing prices throughout the land'. An interesting social comment.

1860

So, with local enthusiasm rising, the work progressed steadily during 1860.

There were few incidents of note during the year and nearly 1,600 men and 70 horses were employed on the line. However, local stories, handed down, tell of what was seen as appalling cruelty to the horses, a feature that did not go down well in a rural community. If these stories are correct, many horses were slaughtered and replaced.

On 18th May, an event of considerable importance took place. Mr D. Campbell, the Resident Engineer of the line, was given the honour of fixing the final keystone in the last archway to be completed on the Ingleton viaduct. This splendid work was built without either loss of life or broken limbs; a remarkable achievement.

1861

Another year passed and by July the work was as good as finished. The entire track had been laid, apart from one of the junctions at Lowgill and those at Ingleton. During July, Errington tested all the bridges with two heavy locomotives and ascertained that the structures were sound. A shortage of labour resulted in some of the station interiors being unfinished but somehow extra men were found and the work completed.

Tuesday 27th August was chosen for the official inspection and this was carried out by Colonel William Yolland, a man who was later to become the Chief Inspector of Railways at the Board of Trade. The whole proceedings aroused considerable local interest and a large number of people turned out to see the inspection, particularly on the large bridge near Sedbergh. Six and sometimes seven locomotives were used without any defects being found and the Waterside viaduct over the River Lune withstood a rolling weight of 250 tons, with three engines and their tenders on each track simultaneously.

After the inspection, Colonel Yolland expressed complete satisfaction and the line was ready for public use.

On 30th August, at the second half-yearly meeting of the shareholders, the Chairman commented with satisfaction that the line was near to opening and that on the table there was an advertisement for the running of goods trains. Errington made a final report on his work during the previous months. The line was his last major work; he died the following year.

Developments in Company politics

Whilst the line had been under construction, several important moves had been made in railway circles. The LNWR had gained control of the branch following, as mentioned previously, the arrangement it had made with the L&C in leasing the latter. Equally important in influencing future events was the fact that the NWR had passed into the control of the MR. The MR had taken the step of laying a double line from Clapham to Ingleton and reopened this section. Clearly the MR was anticipating the inauguration of the through route to Scotland over the line from Ingleton to Lowgill according to what had been deemed desirable by the Parliamentary Committee. However, after the affair involving the 1856 Bill, the MR had turned to the GNR and moved away from the LNWR. In fact by 1860 the LNWR and MR were certainly not on amicable terms!

As far as the line from Ingleton to Lowgill was concerned, this became very apparent over the matter of Ingleton station. The companies had not been able to reach an agreement over the use of the existing Midland Station on the Ingleton side of the viaduct. As a result the LNWR had Thornton station (to become known as Ingleton Thornton) built on the opposite side of the viaduct. The result was that Ingleton had two stations on the same line with less than a mile between them. This turned out to be just a preliminary move in the determination on the part of the LNWR to try to put an end to any notion that the Ingleton to Lowgill section would become part of an effective route to Scotland which might challenge its existing west coast route from Euston.

The line opens

With something of a shadow over the possibility of a Scottish route in the offing, the line was opened to passenger traffic on Monday 16th September, 1861. By this time the line was referred to officially as 'The Ingleton Branch' and timetables referred to it as such. (The use of the term 'branch' in itself might have sounded ominous.)

Although, locally, the event was an occasion for considerable celebration, away down in Euston it was not seen fit to make a song and dance about it. No official celebrations were arranged. There were no festivities and junketing which so often accompanied the opening of a new section of railway in this period; no special inaugural train festooned with bunting and flags. Perhaps Euston was making a statement.

The first train left Ingleton and arrived in Sedbergh at 8.48 am. One of the newspaper reporters present noted that W.A.F. Saunders was on the train. The man who might well have figured prominently in an opening ceremony had to be content to be merely a passenger. At least the town band from Kirkby Lonsdale made an effort to jolly up the proceedings and came over to Sedbergh station to give some sort of sense of occasion to the event.

So, after 15 years of indecision and intrigue, plans and counter plans, Parliamentary Bills and counter-Bills, the line at last was open.

One reporter wrote the following:

> We trust the bickering of the two great rivals, the London and North Western Railway and Midland Railway may soon be at an end and the public treated in the way they deserve. The Act of Parliament under which the line has been constituted is imperative as to the facilities it was intended to afford; and we trust that an amicable management will obviate the necessity for any unpleasant steps being taken.

Unfortunately his hopes were never to be fully realized.

A gravestone in the Parish Church of Sedbergh. It shows the grave of Thomas Nicholson – an Inspector of Works. Note the use of the name 'Lune Valley Railway' a popular description used locally. *Author's Collection*

The 8.48 freight train from Tebay to Clapham at Lowgill Junction on 4th September, 1964. A good view of the junction box seen from the footplate of No. 43029 with the Ingleton Branch bearing left.
M. Covey-Crump

No. 70, a Fowler 2-6-2T class '3P' at Lowgill Junction on a local stopping train to Clapham. Note the main line wooden platform shelter with curved roof, compare with the photograph on page 49.
J.E. Kite

An Interlude

A journey down the line

On leaving Ingleton Thornton, in the County of North Yorkshire, the train would soon pass over the road (now the A65) linking, among other places, Kendal, Settle and Skipton. The steady pace would give the traveller time to take in the gentle pastureland scenery which the line passes through in this part of the journey; sheep and cattle would abound. The first stop would be at Kirkby Lonsdale station. A county boundary had been crossed and now the train would be in Lancashire. The traveller would see little or nothing of Kirkby Lonsdale itself (incidentally, in Westmorland) because the station was some two miles from the town. Following this stop, as the train continued on its journey, the line turned in a more northerly direction. Undulating scenery now begins to appear and when the train reached the next station, Barbon, the traveller would be in the County of Westmorland. As the train left Barbon it would cross the only level crossing on the route and if this journey had been made in the late 1950s or early 1960s, the traveller might possibly spot a milk tanker waiting to cross on its way to the nearby dairy.

Thereafter, the line would continue along the edge of Barbon Fell and then Middleton Fell. Eventually the train would cross over the Sedbergh – Kirkby Lonsdale road on a bridge just before Middleton Head and if the journey was being made before 1931, the train might stop at Middleton station. Just after this stop the traveller with a keen eye and who was looking out of the right-hand side of the forward direction of the train, might catch a glimpse over the low embankment of 'The Railway Tavern' only a short distance from the track. Shortly afterwards the train would cross another bridge over the Sedbergh road and once over this bridge would then pass along the edge of Holme Fell. The traveller who was not admiring the scenery beyond, might just catch a glimpse of the River Rawthey as the train passed over what was often referred to as Jackdaw viaduct.

The line would now begin to follow a semi-circular path which would, after it had crossed a further bridge on the Sedbergh road, passed through Borrett cutting and crossed over the road from Sedbergh to Kendal, bring it to Sedbergh station. When the train reached this station it had, once more, crossed a county boundary and was now in the West Riding of Yorkshire. Again, little would be seen from the train of this market town as the station was a mile or so from it. Moving on, the traveller would not fail to miss the very striking scenery in the Vale of Lune and pass over the river on the Waterside viaduct. Soon it would be possible to experience the stunning views across to the Howgill Fells with the River Lune running at the bottom of the valley. The train would eventually pass over the impressive Lowgill viaduct but from the coach the viaduct would not really be apparent although the views from it would certainly catch the traveller's eye. Once over this striking edifice the train, now back in Westmorland, would pull into Low Gill station (Low Gill being the form of the name often used in railway timetables) and although it may well be going on to Tebay, Low Gill would be the end of the journey on the Ingleton Branch. Taking the journey along this comparatively short branch line would have enabled the traveller to visit four counties: The North Riding of Yorkshire, Lancashire, Westmorland and The West Riding of Yorkshire.

An up freight headed by class '5MT' 4-6-0 No. 45418 passing through Lowgill station in June 1960, on the main line. The Ingleton Branch is seen on the right. *J.R. Sugden*

Chapter Four

Relegation to a Rural Branch
1862 to 1876

1862

In August 1862, Robert Lambert issued a statement in the *Westmorland Gazette* to the effect that he had been authorized to sell various items belonging to Samuel Buxton which had been used in the construction of the Ingleton Branch. The sale was to take place at Lowgill, in September, and among the lots there was an eight-year old cart horse.

The railway was, indeed, well and truly finished but the wrangling and disputes were destined to continue for some time.

Events after the opening of the branch indicated that the River Greta and Ingleton viaduct divided two great railway domains, those of the LNWR and the MR. The arrangement of the two Ingleton stations, to some degree, spared the two companies coming into contact (a situation created by the LNWR rather than the MR). There is some dispute about whether or not there were situations when passengers travelling on from Ingleton in the very early days had to change stations and cross over the viaduct, presumably on foot. There are contemporary accounts that suggest this did happen but whether this was the norm seems unlikely because Midland trains did cross the viaduct to enter Ingleton Thornton. There are also tales about the fact there was a competitive element between the two station masters and passengers travelling north in the winter found the Midland waiting room at Ingleton more convivial because the fire was always better stoked and the place much more comfortable than the waiting room 'over the bridge'. Added to this was the inconvenience caused when a station master let a train on his line go if the 'connecting' train was late. In fact it seems that 'connections' only happened by chance because there was no real effort to co-operate in making these possible. A missed train could leave passengers with a very long wait and even, in some cases, an overnight stay in Ingleton.

In the summer months the water supply for the Midland locomotives sometimes dried up during hot, dry spells. When this happened, Midland men had to swallow their pride and go over to the LNWR side of the viaduct to replenish the tanks in their locomotives. It seems that this water was not free of charge, either!

On a lighter note, in the early years, many people took the penny ride over the viaduct between the two stations to glimpse the magnificent view possible from it.

In spite of the optimism in some quarters and counter to the conditions laid down by Parliament, not only did the through trains not appear, a feature which the LNWR blamed on the MR because (it was said) the latter could not agree on the rates to be charged, but, on the other hand, the train services on the Ingleton Branch were poor and, it seemed, deliberately scheduled to prevent good connections with the Midland trains arriving at Ingleton.

To begin with there were only two trains each day in each direction, one in the morning and one in the early afternoon. These were slow trains and quite useless in providing a link in the Scottish route. The trains ran through to Tebay on leaving the branch and the whole journey from Ingleton to Tebay, a distance of about 22 miles, took one hour and ten minutes.

The branch certainly did bring some benefits to the local community other than providing passenger facilities. In Sedbergh, the local coal, mined near Garsdale, was of a very poor quality. It was said that a fire lit in the early morning would burn, or more realistically smoulder, well into the afternoon without any addition of fuel. The fumes given off were, however, extremely sulphurous and very unpleasant. The opening of the branch made it possible for the people of Sedbergh to acquire more easily a better quality of coal mined near Ingleton. Julia Green Vigour points out in her book that Ingleton coal actually blazed! The hopes of local farmers were realized as well because butter, made in the Sedbergh district, found its way to Leeds. It is reported that by 1862 about seven tons of butter were being taken out by rail each week.

Although (in 1862) the LNWR slightly altered the timetable for the branch to ease, if not to actually facilitate, the connections with the MR for the traveller to Scotland, the MR was far from satisfied.

During the next two years both passenger and freight traffic were seriously impeded by the awkward attitude of the LNWR in the manner in which it dealt with the transfer of traffic when it moved onto the Ingleton Branch en route for Carlisle. The effect was felt even further afield. Freight delayed by the LNWR from Midland lines was impeded in its connection with the Glasgow and South Western (GSWR). Similarly, traffic travelling in the opposite direction from the GSWR and the North British Railway, suffered delays when passing over the Ingleton Branch in the 'care' of the LNWR.

As a result of this and the considerable number of complaints by passengers and operatives, the Midland began to think in terms of abandoning the Ingleton Branch and constructing its own line into

Carlisle. This decision was not made officially until after considerable discussions had taken place about the use of the Ingleton Branch by the MR in conjunction with the LNWR.

These discussions started towards the end of 1863.

1864

At the half-yearly meeting of the L&C shareholders on Tuesday 23rd February, Hassel, the Chairman, commented on the impending agreement between the LNWR and MR companies, stating that it was 'an agreement in which this company is greatly interested'. He pointed out the, by then, well known fact, that the Midland had for some time been anxious to carry its traffic through into Scotland but had given considerable thought to the construction of a line to rival their line. Bearing in mind that the LNWR was leasing the L&C, the latter was very concerned about the possibility of a line which would rival theirs and they had themselves approached the Midland company and had made a proposal which it hoped might have eased the situation relating to the use of the Ingleton line. In this way, the L&C hoped it might avoid the building of a line which would result in competition. Hassel then went on to say he was glad the two companies, namely the LNWR and MR were now 'coming to their senses and instead of setting up rival lines against each other and entering into a mutual destructive competition (a statement which over-exaggerated the case as events were soon to tell) they were coming to terms amicably together which would be a great deal better for the shareholders'.

Hassel then revealed that the previous autumn some of the L&C Directors had had a meeting with Richard Moon, the Chairman of the LNWR. Moon had suggested that the L&C should enter into a new lease with the MR and LNWR companies and have a guaranteed dividend of 9½ per cent. Some of the Directors had considered this to be too low and further negotiations had broken off. Hassel conceded that had 10 per cent been offered, this might have been accepted. Further, Hassel told the shareholders that as a result of the interview with Moon, the LNWR was trying to get a Bill through Parliament to enable it to make the arrangements it sought with the Midland. The effect of this Bill would give the MR a joint interest in the lease of the L&C to the LNWR.

When the Bill came out, a request was sent to the Board of the L&C asking the Directors to call a meeting of the shareholders to consider whether it was advisable to petition against the Bill. Hassel informed the meeting that the petition was ready for presentation and he requested that the Directors be asked to petition against the Bill and to take other such steps as they deemed expedient to protect the interests of the company.

After the motion had been seconded, Mr Bancroft, a representative of the LNWR, spoke for his company. He no doubt felt that the L&C was over-stepping the mark and he pointed out that the Bill was to their advantage as well as the LNWR and MR. He emphasized that his company would not expect the L&C to raise obstacles for the LNWR and moved an amendment to the motion. This amendment proposed that the steps taken by the Directors should be only for the purpose of preserving intact the terms and conditions of the lease.

After considerable discussion, the amendment was lost and the original motion was carried, the result being that the L&C decided to oppose the LNWR Bill in Parliament.

However, by August, the LNWR obtained powers to enter into agreements for the Midland to use the L&C and in November the Midland deposited a Bill for the powers to be put into effect.

Once more, the plans were only short lived. Before a final agreement and settlement could be reached, another dispute arose between the two companies (namely, the LNWR and MR) which time would show, could not be resolved.

The point at issue became the amount of freedom each company should have over the Ingleton line and the L&C system to Carlisle. The MR claimed it should have equal rights with the LNWR and also the right to fix its own charges for traffic to Scotland over its own and the L&C line.

The LNWR agreed to this in principle but pointed out that any Midland traffic actually stopping at a station on the L&C should be charged at a rate agreed by both companies. However, the LNWR classified Carlisle as a station on the L&C and as most of the traffic from the MR or destined for the MR system would almost certainly have to stop at Carlisle, the LNWR was, in effect, forcing the MR into negotiating rates for traffic, thereby robbing it of any freedom to fix its own rates. The MR, unwilling to accept these terms, withdrew from the scheme.

There followed a major development and one which would eventually reduce the Ingleton line to a rural railway branch.

At the beginning of August, the MR gave its Engineer, Crossley, the go-ahead to plan an independent line into Carlisle from Settle.

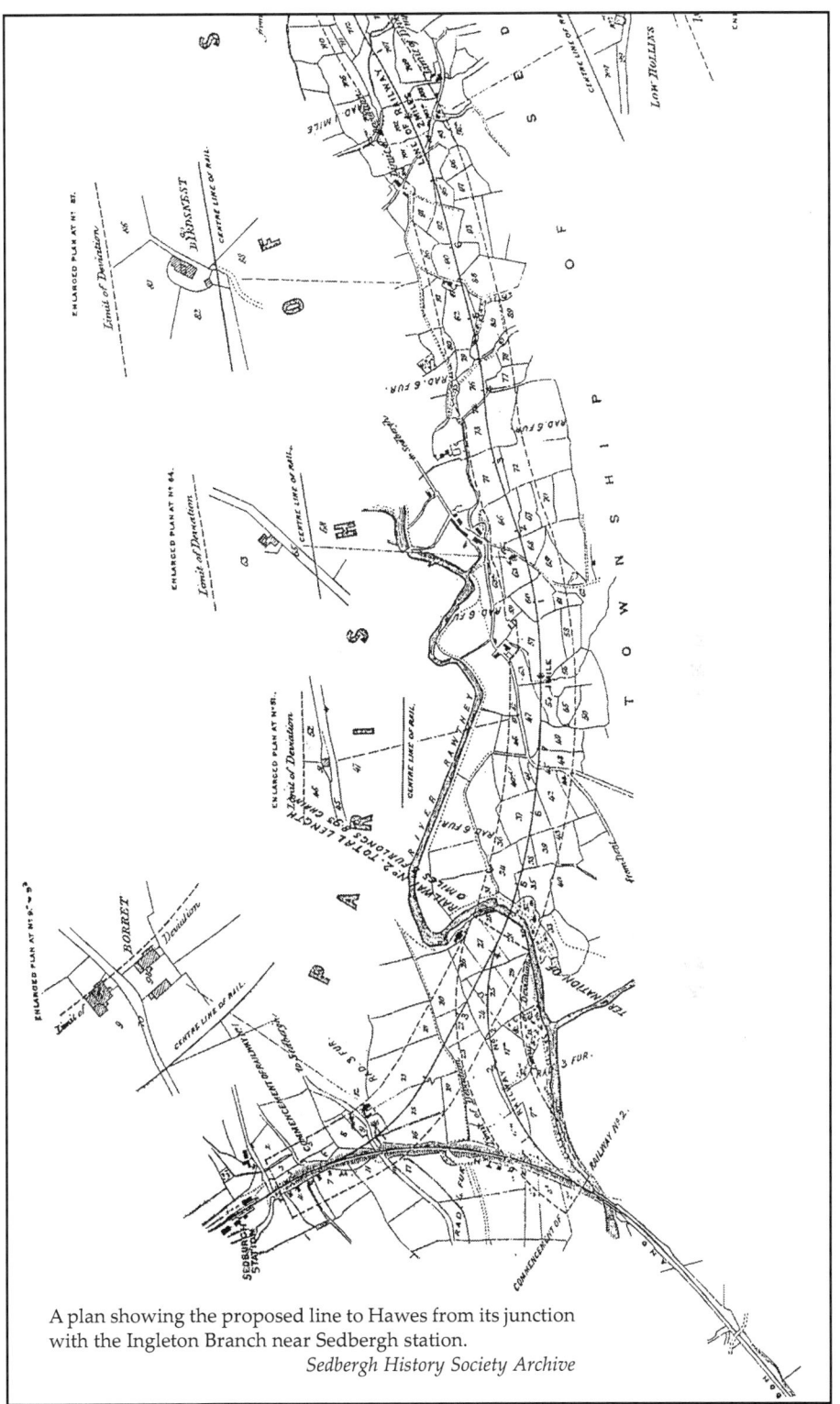

A plan showing the proposed line to Hawes from its junction with the Ingleton Branch near Sedbergh station.
Sedbergh History Society Archive

A further railway link for Sedbergh is proposed.
The Sedbergh – Hawes Railway

Whilst all this was taking place, a development occurred which may have given the Ingleton Branch a more prominent place on the railway system. On Wednesday 5th October (1864) a meeting was held in the Oddfellows' Hall in Sedbergh. The worthies of the town were joined by others including those from Hawes, Leyburn and Masham, together, reports indicate, 'with a large number of landowners and others'. It seems there had been a considerable amount of activity to the east, in Wensleydale, about the provision of railway facilities in that area. The chairman of the Sedbergh meeting was the vicar, The Reverend G. Platt, and he introduced Mr F. MacNay and Mr Smith (who was a Westminster solicitor). MacNay was the Engineer and Smith the solicitor for a proposed new company which would be called 'The East and West Yorkshire Railway Company'.*

They described an outline plan to build a line which 'would not ignore Sedbergh, as other proposed schemes had done, but would commence at Sedbergh station of the Ingleton Branch of the London and North Western Railway and run from thence via Garsdale and Wensleydale to Leyburn and from thence via Masham to Melmerby Junction'. It was suggested that the estimated cost of £8,500 per mile would cover all expenses and could well result in a dividend of 6 per cent. Local support was called upon and the tone of the meeting seemed to be very much in favour of the plan and several of those present went as far as to offer their services as members of a provisional committee.

1865

The year opened on a sombre note, in January, with a fatal accident at Barbon station and an engine driver being accused of manslaughter. An engine returning from Ingleton, having dropped off a goods train, ran into a workers' van. During the inquest, held at the Black Bull in Sedbergh, it was decided by the jury that there were extraneous circumstances and the driver, Henry Burchall, was described as a man of 'excellent character'.

---

* A similar title had been used previously. In 1846 'The East and West Yorkshire Junction Railway Company' was set up but this title was later dropped when, after various mergers, it passed into 'The York and North Midland Company'.

In February there were further misgivings at a meeting of the NWR shareholders when, on 25th February, the Chairman explained that there were still no satisfactory through trains on the line and the Midland seemed reluctant to exercise its powers to rectify this. It was pointed out that 'until it does, the traffic of the NWR will remain underdeveloped'.

Further afield, an Act was granted for the construction of the Hawes and Melmerby Railway. It would seem this altered the intentions of the original scheme put forward in the meeting in Sedbergh the previous year and the proposal now became one to effect a link at Hawes. This new proposal led to Shaw, together with Wyatt and Metcalfe, Parliamentary Agents, to give notice on 14th November of the intention to make to Parliament in the following session (1866) leave to bring in a Bill and to pass an Act to incorporate a company to *'make and maintain'* this railway, now being referred to simply as 'The Sedbergh and Hawes Railway'. The plans were prepared by Nimmo and MacNay. The scheme proved to be a very ambitious one, not least in the demands that were being made in the terms that it outlined relating to other railway companies, including the LNWR.

The powers the new company was seeking were very far reaching. As far as the connection with the Ingleton Branch was concerned there would be, in effect, a forked junction, giving north and south access onto the line. These sections were designated Railway No. 1 and Railway No. 2. Railway No. 1 provided the northerly connection and commenced just to the south of Sedbergh station. Railway No. 2, the southerly junction, would join the Ingleton line just to the north of the bridge over the River Rawthey, thereby avoiding a further structure needed to cross the river. The terms in the proposed Bill made a number of demands. The new company would have the use of all the facilities of Sedbergh station including the booking hall and those of the adjoining yard. This would be at an agreed sum for this use, or failing this, one set down by the Board of Trade. There were conditions relating to the provision of *'direct and speedy transmission of traffic passing to, from or over all parts of the intended Railways of the London and North Western....'* (Perhaps there was an awareness of the problems the MR had already encountered in its dealing with the LNWR!) There were many other clauses about the purchasing of shares by other companies and a section outlining the *'altering, amending, enlarging, extending and, if necessary, repealing the power and provision'* of some Acts with over 30 of these relating to the LNWR alone, together with a large number, in addition, which had a bearing on the NER and the MR.

1866

There is no mention in any of the Parliamentary records of a Bill being presented for 'The Sedbergh and Hawes Railway' although there is a passing mention of it in *'The Reports of Board of Trade on Railway and Canal Bills'*, simply giving the distance as '17 miles 0 chains' but no further mention is made of it.

In the *'Return of Capital in Shares and Loans proposed to be raised by Railway and other Bills'*, the Sedbergh and Hawes Railway Company has listings for returning *'by shares £160,000 and by loans £53,000'*.

Perhaps the decision not to present a Bill was influenced by what was happening elsewhere and which promised to provide a better way forward. The proposal to take a line as far as Sedbergh would appear to have become unnecessary; it looked as though there would be a closer link in the offing at Garsdale when the Settle to Carlisle line had been built. However, this apparent decision not to proceed with the Bill, given the events which followed, lead to something of a 'touch and go' situation two years later, as will be seen.

The MR scheme from Settle to Carlisle, mentioned earlier, had been encountering a difficult passage, both with the shareholders and, later, in Parliament. In spite of this, the Bill was eventually passed in Parliament and became an Act during the session in 1866. Much of the evidence given in support of the line being built centred on the inadequate way in which traffic on the Ingleton Branch had been dealt with by the LNWR. After this evidence had been heard both in the Commons and the Lords, in which the LNWR came off very badly, the Bill received the Royal Assent and became an Act on 16th July.

The NWR was not at all pleased. At the second half-yearly meeting on 29th August, the Chairman, H.J.Hare, commenting on the MR company's power to make a railway from Settle to Carlisle, pointed out that traffic would leave the NWR at Settle once the new line was completed and not at Ingleton. This would be to the detriment of the NWR. He added 'Had the Octuple Agreement never been made, and supported by the Midland Company, a legitimate arrangement would long since have been secured for their traffic to pass over the Lancaster and Carlisle system'*.

Another company which was not at all happy about the Midland Bill was, of course, the LNWR. It would seem the LNWR had overplayed its obstinacy north of Ingleton and had exhausted the patience of the Midland Company. Certainly a line to Carlisle operated independently by the MR could well reduce LNWR receipts for traffic to Scotland by taking some of it out of that company's hands. Now, it seemed, what was needed was a more conciliatory approach and in this mood the LNWR approached the MR with a view to a further attempt to reach some sort of an agreement over the L&C line from Ingleton to Carlisle. It would seem that those who wished to link Hawes to a line which would make it possible to move commodities north and south now had the chance of a better option that taking a line to Sedbergh.

1868
Richard Moon intervenes

In January Richard Moon, the Chairman of the LNWR, and by all accounts a rather formidable person to deal with, wrote to the Midland Company and pointed out the plain facts. The MR would have to spend about £2 million on a line from Settle to Carlisle and the company would need £5 per cent per annum to make it pay. On the other hand, his company was now prepared to accept a net toll of £50,000 per annum for the use of the Ingleton to Carlisle section of the L&C line. Further, the LNWR was prepared to accept this route as a line within the English and Scottish Agreement.

After the very stormy period from 1866 to 1868, relating to the proposed Settle to Carlisle line, which many of the shareholders opposed, and, also, trouble over a proposed amalgamation with the GSWR which was also opposed by a large proportion of the shareholders, the MR seized on the proposals of the LNWR.

---

* The Octuple Agreement, as the name implies, involved eight railway companies. These were the LNWR, the L&CR, the CR, the MR, the GNR, the York Newcastle and Berwick Railway, the York and North Midland Railway and the North British Railway. It was set up in the early part of 1850 after a series of secret negotiations, following the downfall of George Hudson, the so called 'Railway King', in 1849, and the uncertainty which ensued. The driving force behind setting it up was the LNWR, under Mark Huish, the General Manager. The motive of that company was to use its influence within the Agreement to its own advantage, given the aggressive stance this company was wont to make, especially in this period, when it perceived it was under threat from other companies, not least the MR and the GNR relating to the matter of Anglo-Scottish traffic. The purpose of setting it up was ostensibly to arrange for the pooling of traffic and in this way the LNWR sought to exercise control, as it did initially. It disadvantaged the NWR because the Agreement only applied to existing routes and so the NWR would not benefit if and when the Settle to Carlisle line was built. There followed a series of further 'developments' among the companies with some very questionable procedures which eventually led to the downfall of Mark Huish. These developments included possible mergers involving first the LNWR and MR and then the MR and GNR. The NWR saw these activities as being to the disadvantage of its company, hence the comment by the chairman.

Nevertheless, the situation did give rise to something of a dilemma for the Midland company. To accept the offer made by the LNWR, would mean seeking Parliamentary sanction to abandon the Settle to Carlisle project and some of the work had already started.

On the other hand, if Parliament did not approve the proposal to abandon the construction of the line, after what might be a lengthy Parliamentary procedure, the Midland might find itself with insufficient time to build the line in the period stipulated. Further, it might have problems acquiring land because the period for compulsory purchase was rapidly running out.

By November the LNWR and the MR had reached an agreement, subject to the abandonment being approved.

During these deliberations there had also been local objections to the Midland proposal to abandon the scheme. In Appleby, Admiral Russell Elliot, who had been a key proponent in the planning and building of the Eden Valley Railway from Kirkby Stephen up to Penrith, was so keen to get a second railway for the county town that he formed a committee to petition for the retention of the proposal.

1869
Parliament decides

After a very lengthy Parliamentary session lasting from 8th April to the 16th April the Midland Directors were informed that in view of the evidence, the application to abandon their scheme had been rejected and the company must go ahead and build the line from Settle to Carlisle.

That decision was the death knell of any prospect of the Ingleton Branch becoming part of a main route to Scotland. Its status was soon to drop to that of a rural branch line and it lost its potential as a section of a main artery in the railway system. However this outcome may well have been a cause for relief in 'The Sedbergh – Hawes Railway' company's camp! What proved even better; the Midland undertook to build the link from Garsdale to Hawes.

1873

In spite of the growing threat of competition as building of the line from Settle to Carlisle got underway, there seemed little appetite on the part of the LNWR to improve services on the branch. By 1873 a traveller from

Ingleton could catch the 8.20 am departure. This stopped at all stations along the line and on arriving at Tebay there would be a wait of 1½ hours for a train to the north or 45 minutes for one going south. The next train which left at 2.20 pm was better. The wait at Tebay was 20 minutes for both north and south connections. The 3.44 pm went directly to Tebay. This occasioned a wait of 40 minutes for a train to the north with no realistic connection for the south. The 6.35 pm stopped at all stations and at Tebay there was a waiting time of 10 minutes for a train to the north and a wait of 1½ hours for a train to the south. For the most part these could hardly be seen as adequate connections for a through route.

1876
A major development

By the first half-yearly meeting of the LNWR in February 1876, the line from Settle to Carlisle had been opened to goods traffic for several months (although, not at this point, for passenger traffic). At the meeting, Richard Moon drew attention to various drawbacks to the increased prosperity of his company. By no means was the least of these the diversion to the Midland line of Scottish traffic which had originally passed over their company's line. The fears of 1866 had been realized but no more could be done.

The Ingleton Branch meanwhile settled down to 90 years of a quiet rural existence.

A view of Lowgill station showing Fowler 2-6-2T No. 40067 with a local (3.42 pm) train for Clapham. The main line is on the left. Photographed 21st August, 1952.

W.A. Camwell

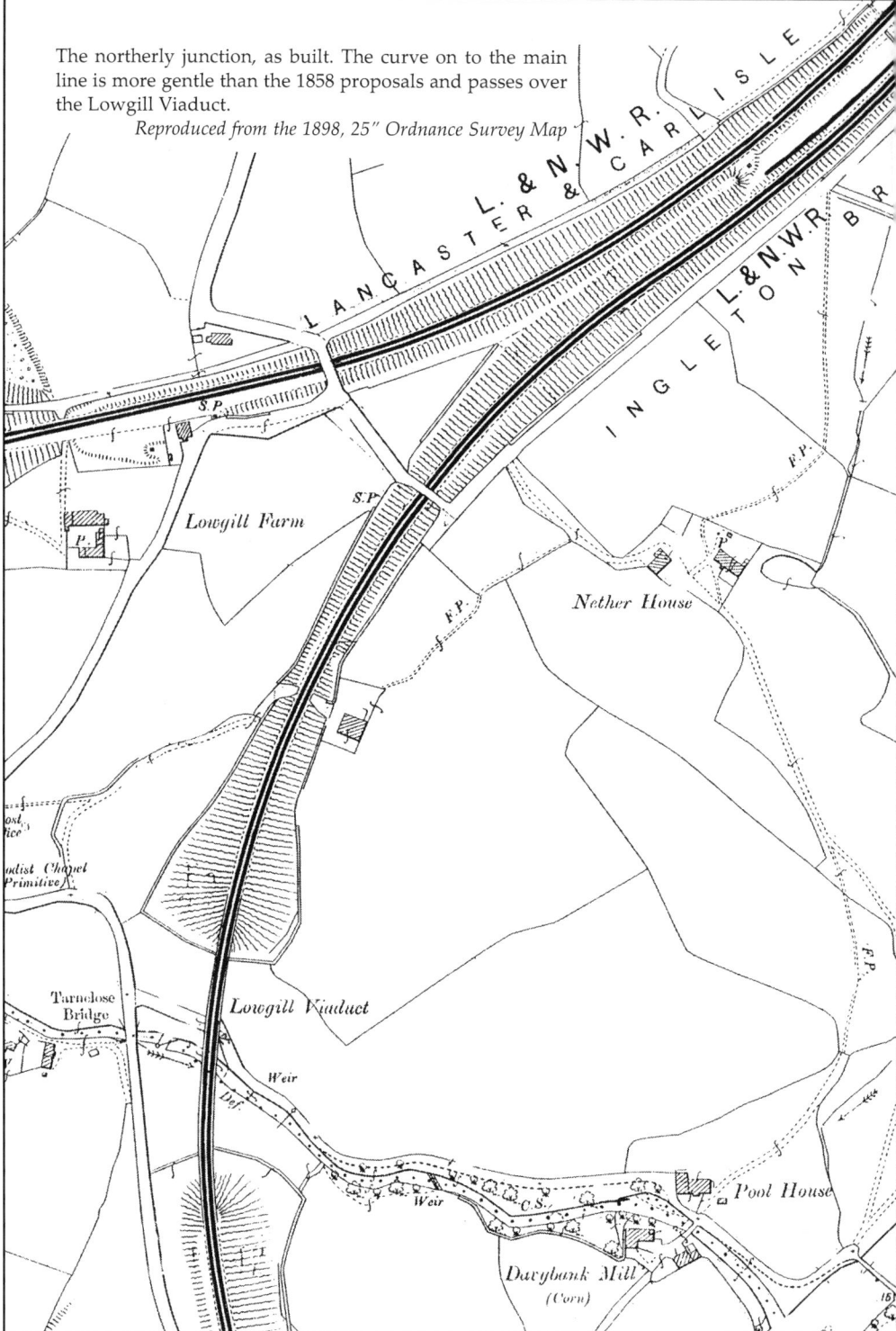

The northerly junction, as built. The curve on to the main line is more gentle than the 1858 proposals and passes over the Lowgill Viaduct.
Reproduced from the 1898, 25" Ordnance Survey Map

The remarkable point of junction at Lowgill. Remarkable because much of the main line is 'duplicated' and the station needed two sets of platforms because it was sited a considerable distance south of the point of junction.
Reproduced from the 1898 25" Ordnance Survey Map

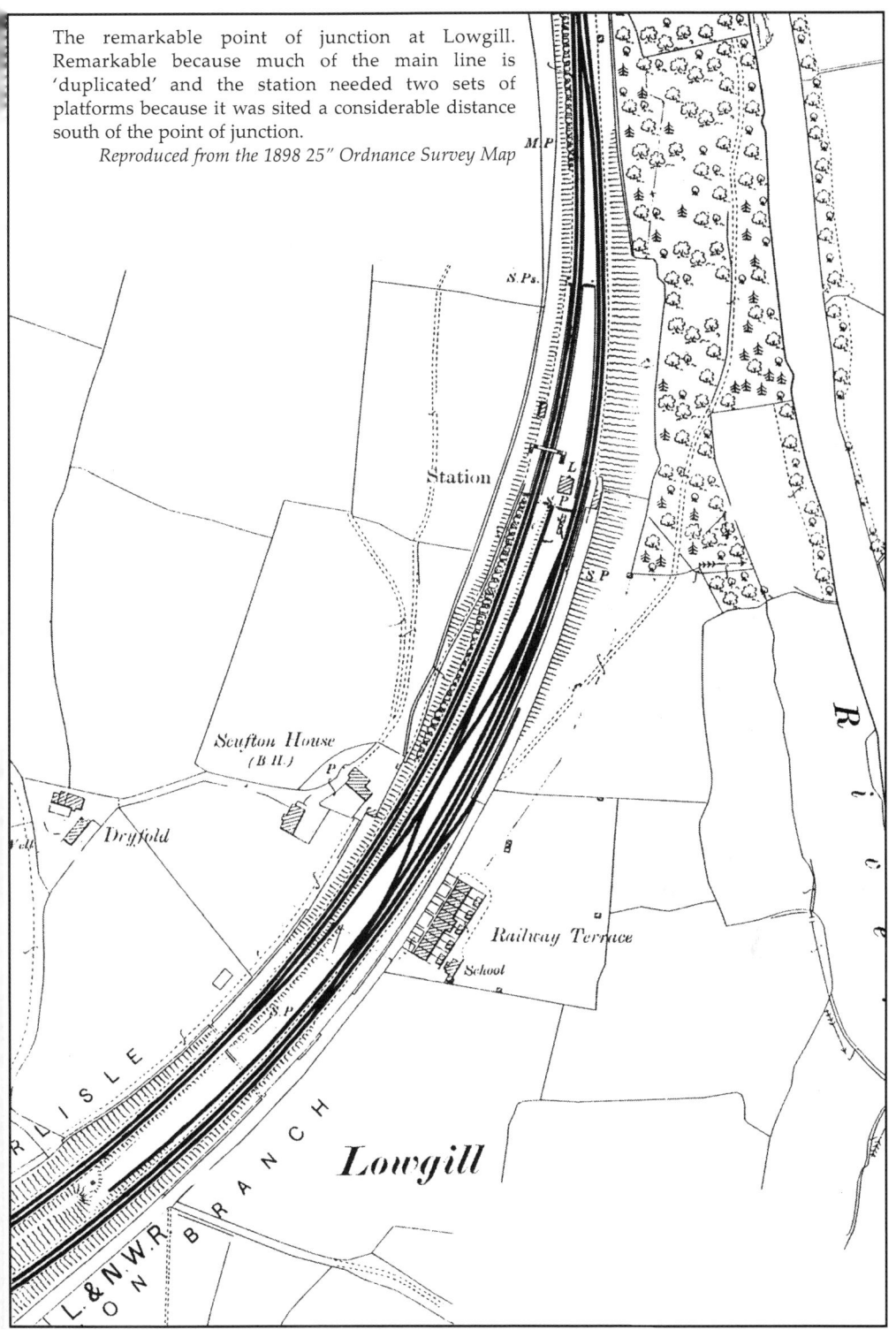

THE INGLETON BRANCH

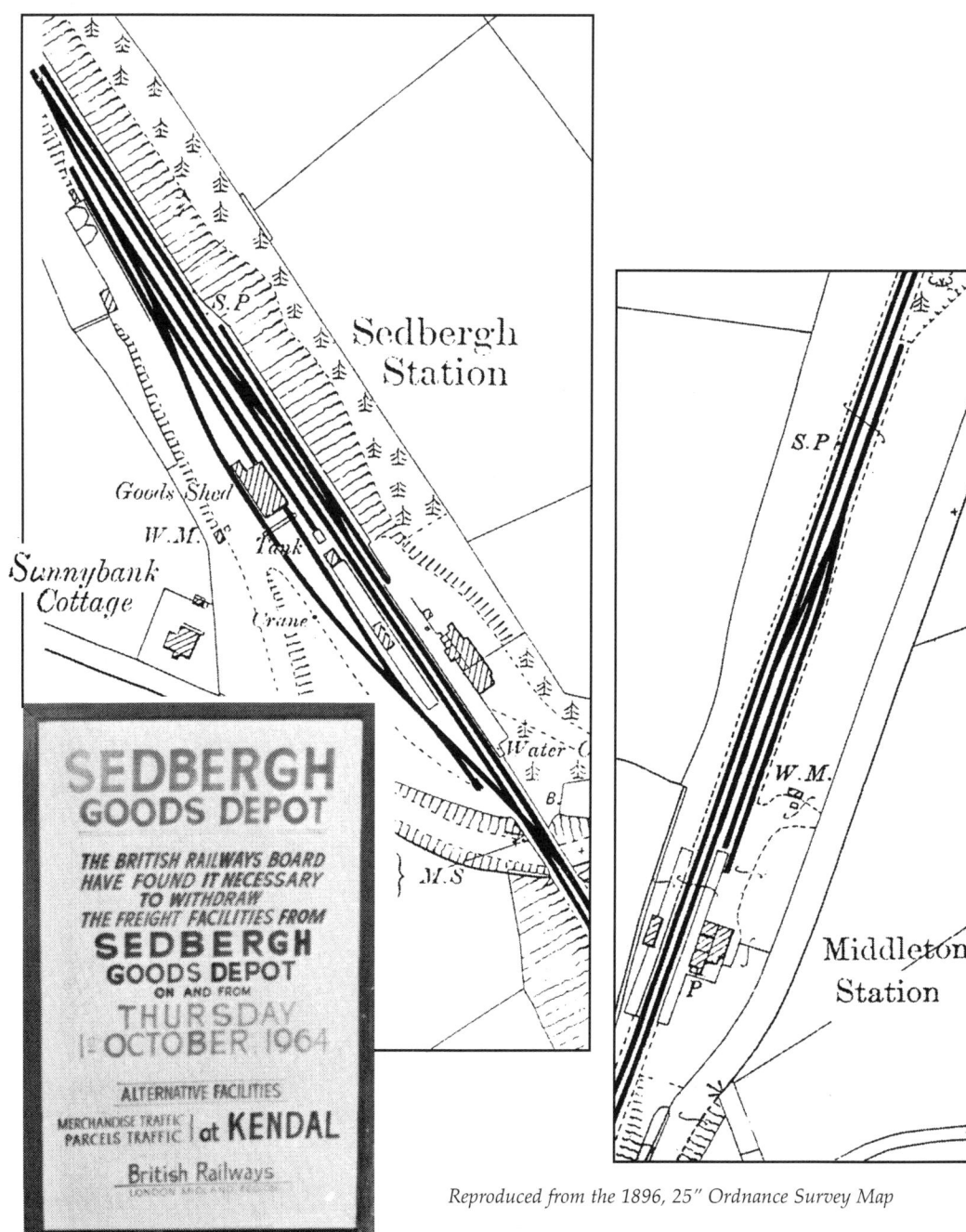

Reproduced from the 1896, 25" Ordnance Survey Map

Chapter Five

The Quiet Years Begin
1876 – 1920

The relationship between a rural branch line and the surrounding district used to be quite different from that with a main line, even when such a line passed through a rural area.

A rural branch line was often part of the community through which it passed and which it served. This was especially so during the last part of the 19th century and the beginning of the 20th when the branch line became a vital link between a small rural community and the world outside. Whilst a main line was busy carrying traffic from one main centre to another, the rural branch could be a local institution. It was often the case that the drivers, firemen and guards along with lineside and permanent way staff, were local people, so adding considerably to the local character of the line. The station master, in a rural community in those early days, was often seen as a pillar of the community and someone who had a special place within it.

The Ingleton Branch was no exception. After all the bickering and inter-company discord, it settled down to serve a particular purpose and it is no exaggeration to say that it was viewed with affection by the folk living in the small communities which it served.

In the period from 1876 to 1964 the line saw little that could be thought of as out of the ordinary; it was simply 'there' enabling local produce to be taken out and other commodities to come in.

Once the keen rivalry of the LNWR and MR had died down a little, there were some improvements in the train services but even so they were very slight.

Although not strictly on part of the Ingleton Branch, a development 'over the bridge' and in the other camp at Ingleton Midland is worthy of a mention.

On 11th April, 1885, the waterfalls in the craggy areas near Ingleton were opened as a tourist attraction. This was achieved by carrying out work which enabled easy access by means of walkways, steps and bridges. A charge was made for entry and the venture was an unqualified success. The fears of some that the coming of the railways might provide greater mobility to large numbers of the populace and so threaten the peace of rural areas might have been realized at Ingleton. However, in this case, it came about with the approval of local people, especially those in trade. Thousands of people travelled by the Midland to see and make these impressive walks. They came during public holidays from Leeds, Bradford, Manchester and places within these areas, being conveyed by a large number of special trains. Ingleton Thornton must have seemed to be a very quiet station indeed.

In addition, Ingleton was a place where coal was mined and as pointed out by Julia Green Vigour, it was of a better quality than that which was mined further up the dale. The colliery, owned by Hunter and Company, provided an important source of fuel for the immediate locality with small quantities being taken further afield. In the 'Report of the Commissioners appointed to inquire into the several matters to coal in the United Kingdom Vol III - Statistics of Production, Consumption and Export (Committee E)' it is stated that 'in 1856 thirty-three tons of coal were carried from the colliery at Ingleton by way of the Midland Railway'. This was insignificant compared to the collieries further south (Colne, for example, took out 4,562 tons). More important was the limestone being quarried. There were two main quarries, Meal Bank Quarry and The Ingleton Granite Quarry. Two mineral lines were built to connect these to the line between Lowgill and Clapham; one went to Ingleton Thornton and the other to Ingleton Midland.

Meal Bank Quarry, which was opened in 1869 by Clerk and Wilson and which was later named The Craven Lime Quarry, was situated on the north-west end of the town. Originally the limestone, after treatment in the Hoffman continuous burning kiln, was taken down to Thornton station yard by horse and cart. This yard was on high ground on the side of the Greta Gorge, spanned by the Ingleton viaduct. Transportation was made difficult as a result because a considerable section of the journey was up a steep slope. As the demand for limestone increased, the quarry owners considered building a mineral line from the quarry to the station yard. This proposal raised concern because the entrance to the Ingleton walks was between the quarry and the station. The proposals included building two bridges linking high embankments and the owners of the walks felt the scheme would detract from the scenic appeal and possibly impair trade by discouraging visitors.

However, the arguments for building such a mineral line were hard to resist. More jobs would be created at the quarry and this, in turn, was expected to bring more trade into the town. Following negotiations, the owners agreed to the line being built and this decision was greeted with considerable enthusiasm locally. The line constructed left Meal Bank Quarry through a short tunnel and then crossed the river onto a high embankment. It then crossed the entrance to the walks on a high iron girder bridge and so on to Thornton station. The line was opened on 13th March, 1893 having taken about a year to build. The track was

Fowler 2-6-2T No. 40067 standing at Lowgill station with the 3.42 pm local service to Ingleton on 21st August, 1952. *W.A. Camwell*

Another cab view from class '4MT' 2-6-0 No. 43029 on 4th September, 1964. Having just left the junction, the train is on the Lowgill viaduct going south. *M. Covey-Crump*

Sedbergh station at the turn of the century, as seen from an early postcard.
John Alsop Collection

A fine view of Sedbergh station, *c.*1900 with ladies and gentlemen in period costume.
Author's Collection

standard gauge and this was necessary because LNWR locomotives needed to have access.

The works closed in 1909.

The other quarry, located to the north-east of Ingleton was eventually worked by ARC Roadstone. This quarry, formerly the Ingleton Granite Quarry, was opened in 1888 by John Scott and Company. The owners also wished to have a mineral line and in their case it had to connect the quarry, about two miles outside Ingleton, with the Ingleton Midland yard. The engineer and contractor for the line was John Hewitson, a resident of Ingleton.

Generous offers were made to the owners of the land through which it was planned the line would pass and once the sections of the land had been purchased, the work, which went ahead quickly, was started in 1887. It was reported that Hewitson was so determined to complete the line in as short a time as possible that 'he did away with horse labour and acquired a locomotive'.

From the quarry there was a single track which passed the stock yard, the reservoir, the White Scar Caves, around the hill at Skirwith, close to Crina Bottom and ended above Easegill. This section of the line, which was about a mile long, was worked by a saddle-tank with the name *Northumbria*. The second section of the line started at Easegill and this was an inclined railway on a gradient of 1 in 6.

At the top of this section there was a large brake drum around which a cable, used for hauling the wagons, was wound. Two loaded wagons were lowered by means of the hawser and these wagons hauled up two empty wagons. This line was single track with a passing loop at the half-way stage, the points for this being spring loaded. The line passed below the Ingleton to Clapham road and at the bottom the wagons were detached and a Midland locomotive took them round the sharp curve and into the Midland yard. The whole system was standard gauge, enabling the same wagons to be used throughout the procedure.

As well as handling stone, the line served another purpose. Each Friday a wagon of coal was taken up the incline. The local farmers then went to Crina Bottom Lane and collected the coal using horse and cart. The coal had to be unloaded by the end of weekend before the railway commenced work on Monday morning.

In 1924, after complaints about the frequency of runaway wagons on the incline, an aerial ropeway was built to transport the stone and this had a capacity to move 10 tons per hour. The inclined railway was then closed.

Still in its LMS livery, Fowler class '3P' 2-6-2T No. 16 stands at Sedbergh station, on 28th August, 1948, with the 6.42 pm service from Clapham to Tebay. Note the passengers crossing the track behind the train.

W.A. Camwell

A view of Sedbergh station after closure looking north, photographed on 10th July, 1965. *H.B. Priestley*

In its heyday about 150 tons were moved out by the railway each day. Much of this stone was destined for Liverpool. With the onset of the First World War the quarry was closed.

Without doubt the prosperity of both these quarries depended on the Ingleton Branch.

[Much of the information about the quarries was provided by Mr J.J.Wilson and Mr J.Slinger of Ingleton and Mr Wilson recounted how his grandfather, who lived at the foot of Ingleborough, collected his stock of coal for the winter in this way.]

1910
The Lake District Express

As far as passenger services were concerned, an interesting development occurred in 1910, involving through services on the branch. In that year the *Railway News* published a report in July stating that a special express train would run between Hellifield and Carlisle over the LNWR through Ingleton and Lowgill. The experimental run was made in order to test the bridges and platforms in readiness for a regular service to be run by the MR over the same route. The service, which was scheduled to start on 1st July, 1910, would connect Leeds and the West Riding and also Nottingham, direct to Keswick.

The timetable for July gives the departure time from Leeds as 10.00 am. A connection facility provided for travellers from London, officially called 'The Lake District Express', meant a very early start at 5.00 am. The train stopped at Nottingham and Sheffield. It ran without stopping after Leeds except, it seems, certainly so in later years, for a change of motive power to an LNWR locomotive at Clapham. It then travelled over the Ingleton Branch to Penrith. Perhaps what is notable is that the LNWR locomotive took over before LNWR 'territory'!

'The Lake District Express' does not seem to have met with a great deal of success because in 1913 it was withdrawn. However, a through train did continue to run from Leeds to Keswick and although the service was suspended during the First World War, it was reintroduced when hostilities ceased.

In spite of these through trains, the line continued to operate with Ingleton dividing the two major operating companies.

Towards the end of the same year there was another event which had repercussions for the branch. In his recollections, Jack Sedgewick, a former resident and bank manager in Sedbergh, recalls an event when he was a small boy. After Christmas he was walking with his father through the fields near Sedbergh and close to the line when they saw Midland trains using the line. His father commented that there must be 'something going on, at the Midland line [The Settle and Carlisle] for those trains to be coming this way'. On 24th December there had been a devastating crash on the Midland line just north of Garsdale; a crash which was so devastating that it would remain in the memory for many years and feature in the history of that part of the Midland Railway.

1914–1918
The First World War

With the onset of the First World War, under 'The Regulation of Forces Act (1871)'the country's railway system was put under Government control from midnight on 4th August, 1914. The result was that for the time being, the line from Clapham up to Lowgill was effectively one entity. The movement of troops and general freight commodities saw no boundaries and there was increased activity especially in a northbound direction. The tonnage increased each year during the war.

It was also during the war, on 22nd January, 1917, that the LNWR announced it would no longer be prepared to carry goods between the station at Kirkby Lonsdale and the town. The distance involved was over 2½ miles. This move caused considerable consternation among the local traders. Road transportation was not a particularly easy business in wartime and the proposed change in facilities was quite a blow. A meeting was called at which it was made clear that for each man to carry his own goods from the station to the town would prove very expensive and so increase the cost of several commodities. It was decided, as a result, to invite tenders from local hauliers although there seems to be no evidence that the matter was taken any further.

A Royal visit

There was at least one occasion when the Royal Train visited the branch.

King George V and Queen Mary visited Sedbergh School on 18th May, 1917 during a tour of north-west England. The train stayed overnight in Borrett cutting, just outside Sedbergh station. Such was the level of security in those days that just one policeman, Constable Dawson, had the job of guarding the train.

A busy Sedbergh station with Fowler class '3MT' 2-6-2T No. 40067 on a local passenger train from Lowgill to Clapham. A northbound goods is seen on the other line, taking water on 21st August, 1952.   *W.A. Camwell*

A fine old postcard of Sedbergh station with passengers and freight awaiting the local service. Note the highly polished milk churns; a thing of the past.   *Oakwood Collection*

Class '5MT' 4-6-0 No. 44963 on a northbound freight (diverted) awaiting the 'right away' at Barbon station, whilst sister engine No. 44673 approaches the stop signal at the level crossing with a diverted southbound freight on 10th March, 1963.

C.B. Metcalfe

Class '4F' 0-6-0 No. 44570 in a snow shower at Barbon station on 17th March, 1963 with another diverted northbound freight from the Settle to Carlisle route.

C.B. Metcalfe

Class '5MT' 4-6-0 No. 44671, fitted with a snowplough, storms through Barbon station on a diverted southbound freight (the Settle to Carlisle route blocked by heavy snow) on 10th March, 1963. (Note the milk tanker waiting to cross the line to the large dairy, which was situated at the side of the station.)

C.B. Metcalfe

THE QUIET YEARS BEGIN

Post war

After the war, services eventually reverted to the pre-war routines. The amount of traffic dropped, the daily freight services resumed and the through train from Leeds to Keswick ran as before.

Just before the war commenced, and reintroduced immediately afterwards, a local service was operated which was intended to cater for people from Sedbergh and Ingleton, together with the surrounding district, returning from Kendal market. It left Kendal at 5.05 pm and was worked by an Oxenholme engine. It first went to Oxenholme. Here there was a reversal and it went down to Lowgill. After a further reversal at Lowgill, it continued to Ingleton. In addition to having passenger facilities the train also included horse boxes and cattle wagons for the convenience of those who had made purchases at the market. The train stopped at all stations en route for Ingleton.

During this period there were some unfortunate incidents on the line. Many local people, particularly at the northern end of the branch, frequently used the line as a footpath, finding it much easier to use than the roads or tracks. A number of those who chose to use the railway in this way were badly injured and, in some cases, fatally so.

There are tales which bear witness to the friendly relationships which existed between the enginemen and the local people. It was not unknown for a farmer to hitch a lift on the footplate of a locomotive to get from one part of his land to another. There are tales of 'Jonty' Foster, one of the local drivers. He was a great friend of the young railway enthusiasts of Sedbergh and district and would allow them on to the footplate. When he collapsed and died on an engine as it approached Barbon, it is said that many felt they had lost a good friend and companion.

Nevertheless, settled though it seemed to have become, as time passed this post-war period would eventually see considerable changes to the railway system in Great Britain.

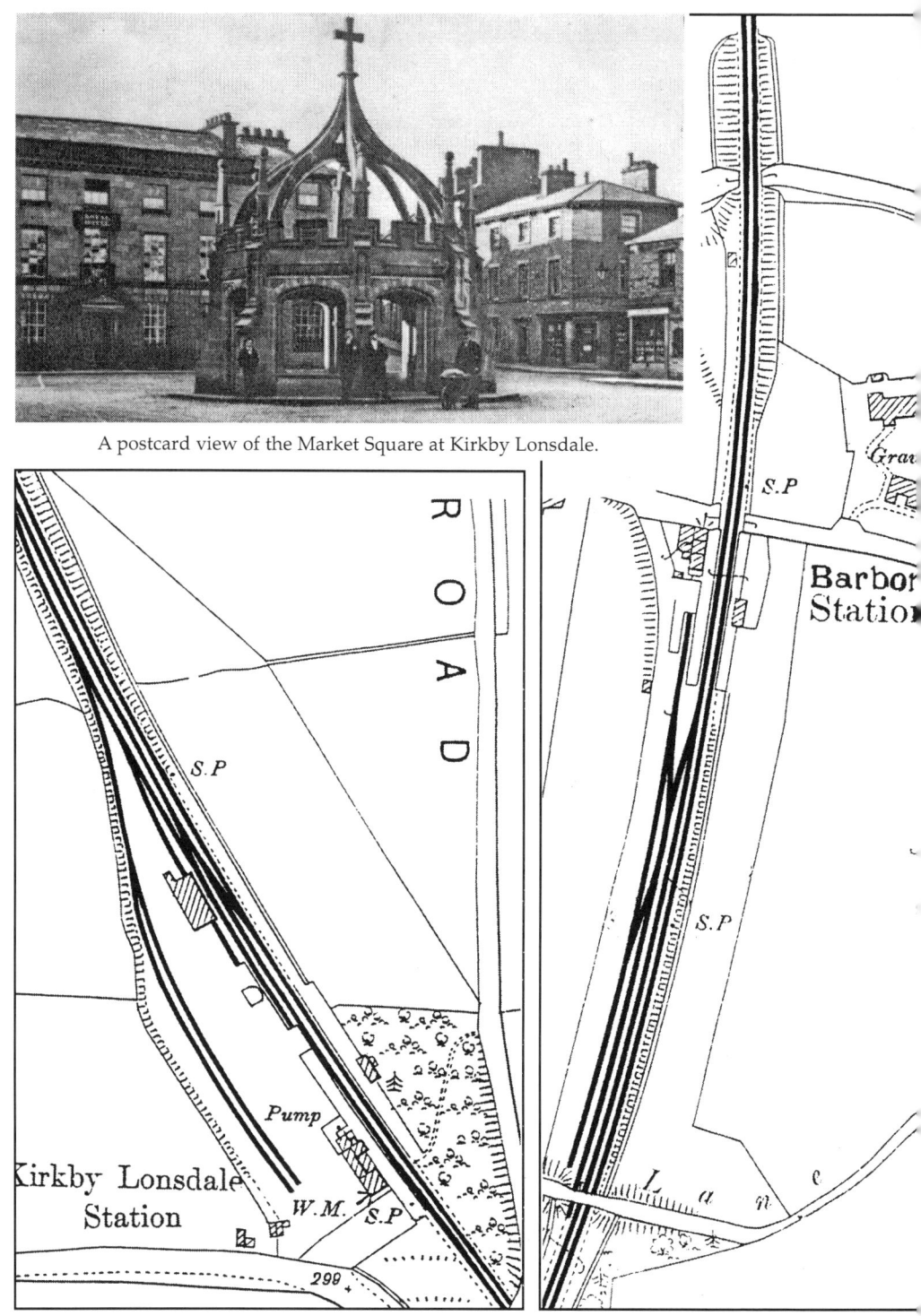

A postcard view of the Market Square at Kirkby Lonsdale.

Reproduced from the 1896, 25" Ordnance Survey Map

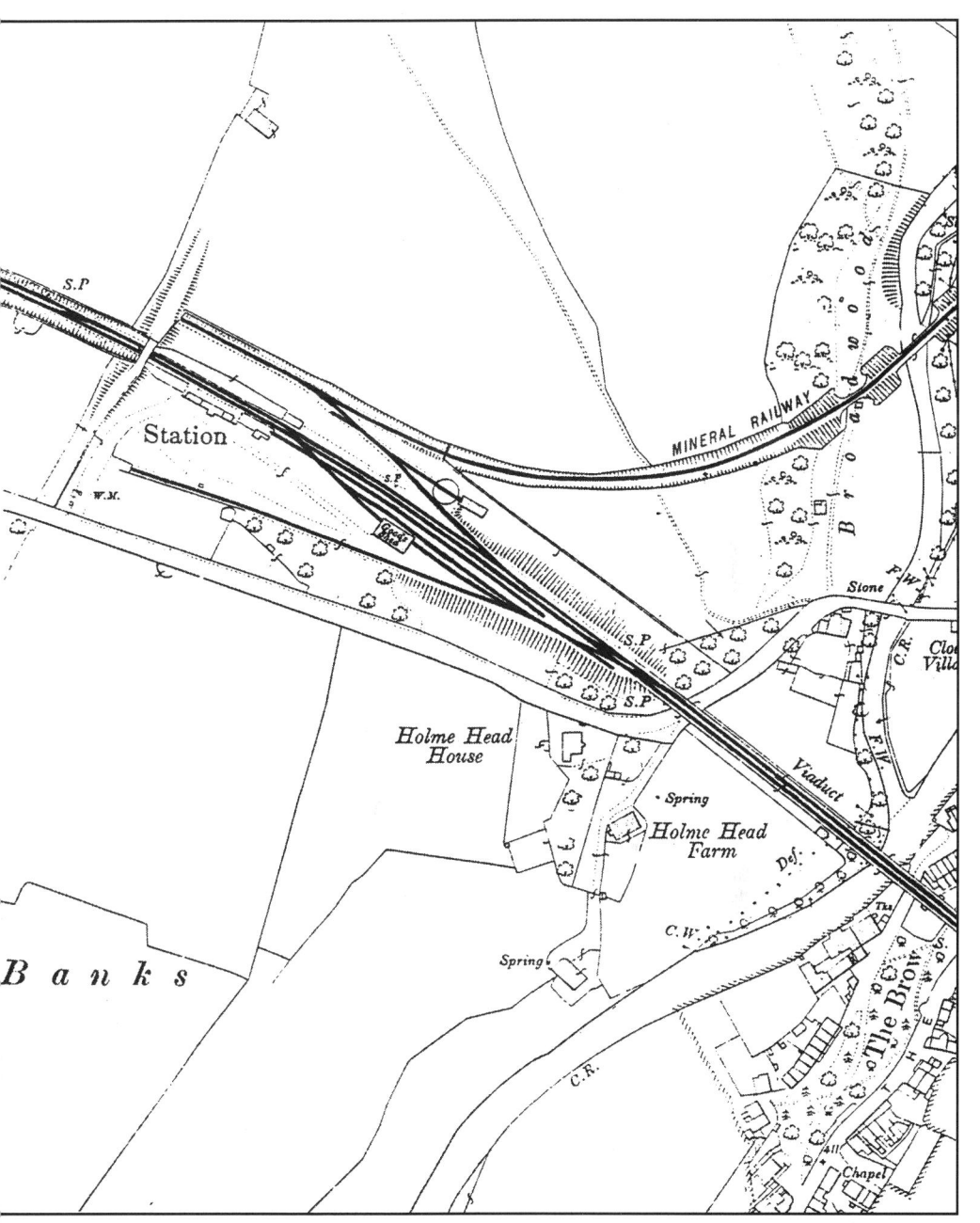

Ingleton Thornton station. *Reproduced from the 1907, 25" Ordnance Survey Map*

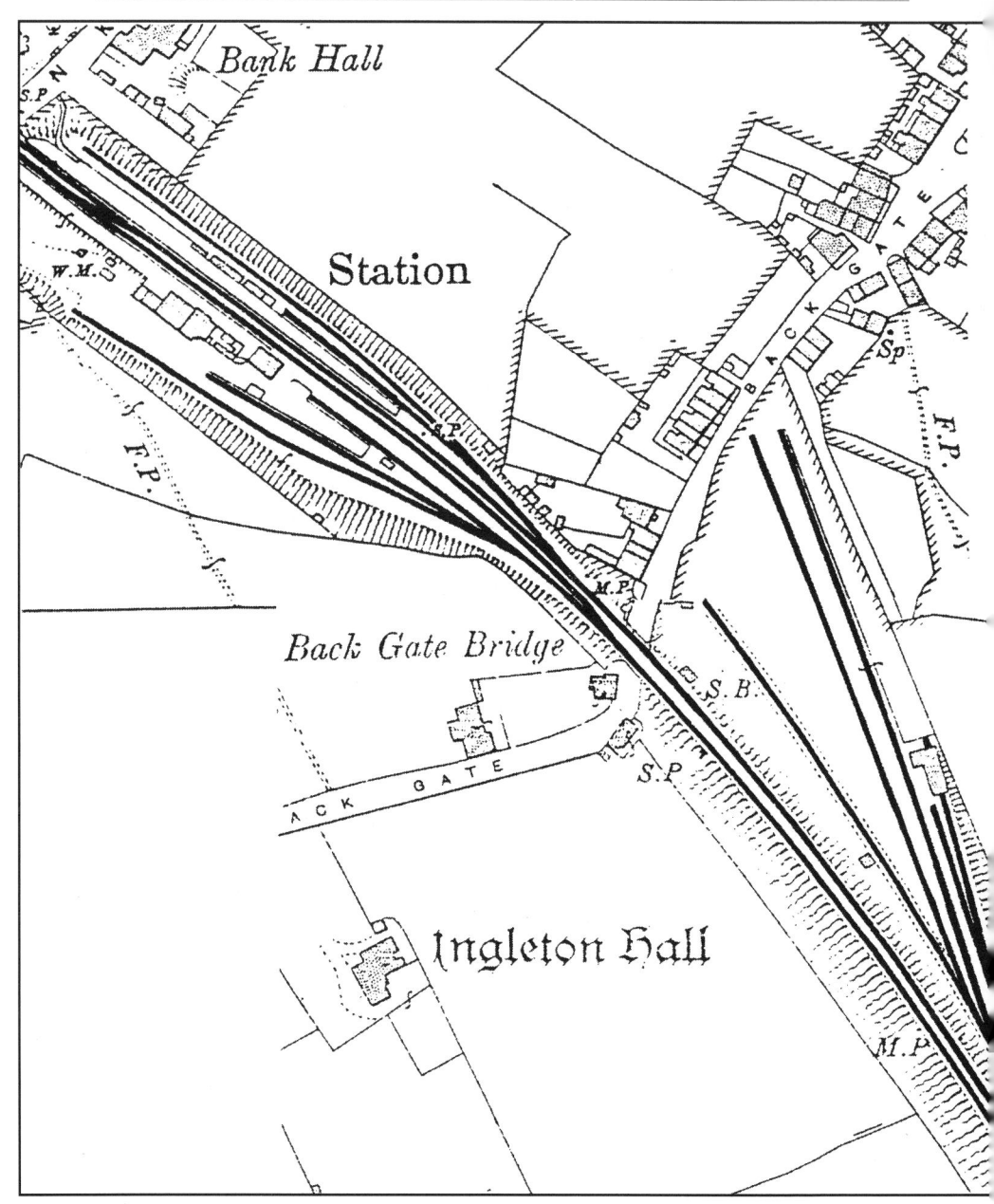

Ingleton Midland station. *Reproduced from the 1907, 25" Ordnance Survey Map*

Chapter Six

A Further Period of Change
1920 to 1948

The Big Four
1922 to 1923

After the First World War was over there had been some uneasiness in the corridors of the major railway companies such as the LNWR and MR about the apparent reluctance of the Government to hand back the lines to their owning companies. There was conjecture about why this might be so but what eventually happened was a radical reorganization of the rail network across the land.

The process was mooted in 1922 and carried forward into 1923 when the new arrangements became finalized.

There had been a feeling that the Government might well decide to hold on to the railway system and keep it under Government control; effectively nationalizing it.

Possibly because the manner in which the war had taken its toll on the infrastructure and a lack of investment in its upkeep and, further, given the costs that would be involved in building it up again, the Government stopped short of making such a move.

Instead it decided to group the national rail system into four main companies, namely The London Midland and Scottish Railway, The London and North Eastern Railway, The Great Western Railway and the Southern Railway.

The result of this amalgamation of the various railway companies would mean that the LNWR and the MR would now be under one roof, namely the London, Midland and Scottish Railway, initially referred to as the LMSR but later simply the LMS.

Old enemies were now brothers – if only by adoption!

The obvious effect that this move had on the Ingleton Branch was to remove the inconvenient 'division' at Ingleton and make the branch a 'unit' from Lowgill to the junction at Clapham. In spite of this, the last train of the day always terminated at Ingleton and the locomotive was shedded there for the night.

The pattern of passenger train working resulted in the first train of the day leaving Ingleton and this went down to Clapham. This train then left Clapham and called at all stations en route for Lowgill. From there the train worked the empty stock to Tebay where fresh stock, which had been cleaned and brought down from Carlisle, was collected. The

Class '5MT' 4-6-0 No. 45347 waiting at Barbon station level crossing with a train of scrap, during the removal of the Ingleton Branch track. Note the up line has already been removed on 24th May, 1967. *F. Dean*

Kirkby Lonsdale station after closure looking north on 10th July, 1965, just two years before track removal. *H.B. Priestley*

engine was replaced by another and this locomotive and the fresh stock went as the next train on the branch, starting at Tebay and going to Clapham. The next train left Clapham but terminated at Ingleton, afterwards retuning to Clapham. This train was followed by one leaving Clapham for Lowgill and then making the journey back. There was a further trip to Ingleton and back to Clapham and the last train down the branch left Clapham and went to Tebay. The final run of the day was from Tebay to Ingleton and after this run the locomotive was shedded for the night. All the trains stopped at all the stations on the branch and the timetable was so arranged that one locomotive and one set of stock could be used throughout.

Excluding the short trips between Clapham and Ingleton only, it can be seen that there were three up trains and three down trains each day. However, an additional train was introduced in the early 1950s following complaints from people in Sedbergh and the surrounding district that the first train to Clapham did not give them an early enough start for a day's outing to Leeds. The result was the introduction of a train leaving Lowgill at 7.10 am, making possible a connection with a Morcambe – Leeds train which stopped at Clapham specially to effect this. For this new service, the stock ran empty from Ingleton to Lowgill and the locomotive ran round the train for the return journey. The arrangement for the daily change of stock at Tebay remained as before.

Following the amalgamation of 1923 it was not felt necessary to have two stations serving Ingleton and so the former LNWR one, Ingleton Thornton, was closed because it was felt the former MR station was better placed for the town. The building was soon razed to the ground but the LNWR yard continued to be used as a coal depot and this continued into the late 1960s.

Middleton station was renamed 'Middleton-on-Lune' following the Grouping, but not for long. It soon became apparent that there was little use for this station, Middleton being an area of scattered farms and seemingly with no community nucleus. This station was the second on the branch to be closed to passengers and closure came on 4th April, 1931. The block signalling equipment was moved to Sedbergh. In fact there were no signal boxes on the LNWR portion of the line and all the block signalling equipment used was sited at the various stations.

The building at Middleton was not demolished and still remains. After the station was closed and whilst the line was still open, a wagon of coal was left at the former yard to facilitate the distribution of this commodity in the locality and save road haulage from Sedbergh.

To all intents and purposes the line settled down to a quiet routine but occasionally there were, ironically, perhaps, Scottish expresses to be seen on the line. The Lune Valley may sometimes remain clear of snow when there are heavy falls in Dent Dale, especially in the Garsdale area, causing severe conditions on the Settle and Carlisle line. In these circumstances the former Ingleton Branch could be used as a relief line for diverting traffic. Several observers noted the appearance of former Midland expresses on the line during the very severe winter in 1962-3.

1934–36
Problems at Lowgill Station
An unusual court case

A court case in 1936 throws light on a practice on the branch section at Lowgill station.

On 14th May, 1936, Mr Justice Smith presided over a case being heard at the Assizes in Leeds involving a claim made against the LMS railway company relating to an incident at Lowgill station two years previously. Edgar Dennis, an engineer from London, had been travelling to Sedbergh on 19th November, 1934 and left the train from Euston at Lowgill in order to travel down the branch. He was alleging breach of contract of duty on the part of the station master and, in turn, the railway company. Given that it was dark, the station master had escorted Mr Dennis across the tracks and to the coach. The arrangement of the platforms on this part of the station at Lowgill had created a situation on some sections whereby the platform level was lower by some two feet than the running board of a coach. In view of this what was referred to as a 'mounting block' was kept in the waiting room and could be accessed, when needed, by the station master or even, it would seem, by a passenger who knew it was kept there. The station master had not informed him of the possible use of a 'mounting block' and simply asked him whether he would be able to step up into the coach.

Mr Dennis had said he thought he could climb into the coach but in trying to do so had slipped and caught his shin on the running board whereupon the station master had pushed him up into the coach. Unfortunately the wound Mr Dennis sustained had turned septic and he was indisposed for some time as a result.

Oddly the judge seemed to make rather light of the whole business.
Judge: 'What year did you say it was?'
Dennis:' The Year of Our Lord 1934. Did your Lordship think I said 1834?'
Judge: 'I thought you said 1634'.

Fowler class '3MT' 2-6-2T No. 40067 seen here at Kirkby Lonsdale station with the 3.42 pm Lowgill to Clapham local service on 21st August, 1952. *W.A. Camwell*

Kirkby Lonsdale station buildings as seen from the station yard. The larger part of the building on the left is a domestic dwelling and the smaller section on the right the old waiting room. *Author*

Ingleton station (Midland) seen here on 4th August, 1958, looking north. Note carriage stock stored behind the goods shed. A view of the unusual signal box can be seen.

H.B. Priestley

The same locomotive as on previous page seen here at Ingleton Midland at 4.19 pm on 21st August, 1952.

W.A. Camwell

A FURTHER PERIOD OF CHANGE 73

After what amounted to further banter, the matter of the mounting block was brought up.
Judge: 'It is highly inconvenient for passengers to have to take this stool around with them.'
Dennis: 'There is a wait of three quarters of an hour'
The Judge was shown a photograph of the mounting block.
Judge: 'And they amuse themselves by carrying it up and down?'

For the company Mr Payley Scott said that in his view there was no case to answer. The station had been there for 60 years and passengers had always had to step up onto the train.

After more exchanges during which the Judge expressed the view that passengers crossing the railway lines should be afforded the use of a bath chair, he came down of on the side of Mr Dennis and awarded him £300 and costs.

The Second World War and the aftermath
1939

The onset of the Second World War saw the introduction of an Emergency Passenger Timetable by the LMS.

As far as the Ingleton Branch was concerned the schedule was that at 8.37 am a train left Ingleton for Tebay. This was followed by a 9.10 am from Tebay to Clapham. There was a 6.00 pm from Clapham to Lowgill and then, finally, at 7.40 pm a train from Lowgill back to Ingleton. What might be described as a basic service. The war effort did bring additional traffic onto the branch. The grounds of Ingmire Hall, near Sedbergh, were used for storing petrol and this facility brought special trains which unloaded at either Sedbergh or Middleton.

1945
Desperate measures

After the war ended in 1945 there would soon be changes which were certainly much more significant than those which had occurred after the First World War.

Probably the most far reaching of these was the way in which road transport developed both as far as the carriage of passengers and, especially, freight was concerned. The internal combustion engine was on the ascendancy and gradually the roads were improved in order to cope with this revolution in the country's transport system. Coal and agricultural goods, basic slag and beet pulp, among them, would soon be carried at very competitive rates by road and the heavy lorry became part of the rural scene. Not only this, the war had left the railways in a rather sorry state, inevitably lacking in investment at a certain level because of the war effort. How would the four major companies cope with this? A very substantial amount of capital would be required. In addition to all this there was another change taking place and this was related to political strategies. It involved a policy of public ownership and the railways were no exception when it came to the realization of this mode of thinking.

Only three years after the war had ended the 'Big Four' lost their power and in January 1948 the railways were taken over by the Government; nationalized.

There was conjecture about where this would leave, in particular, rural lines such as the one between Clapham and Lowgill.

This branch had not really had any competitive value after the First World War but it had been able to serve a useful purpose which enabled it to keep going.

Under the new regime the shadow of economic viability began to fall across the system. Lines which were unprofitable would have to go; there was no question about that. As would be seen, later, unfortunately the line from Clapham to Lowgill, The Ingleton Branch, came in this category.

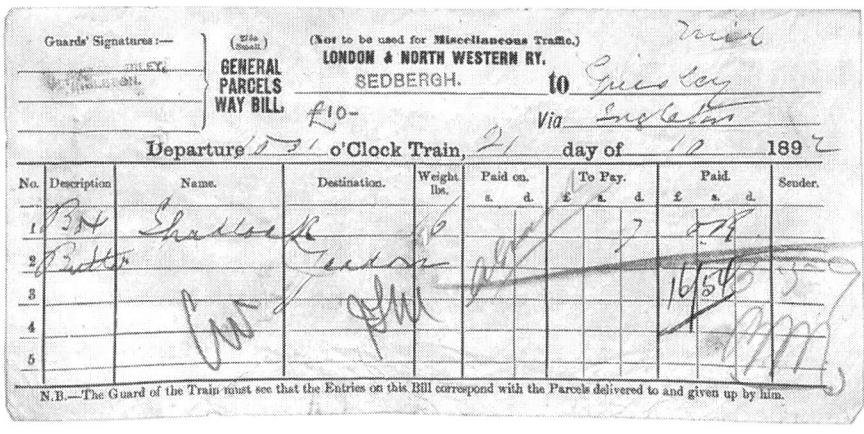

An 1892 parcels way bill, for a box of butter, from Sedbergh Station to Yeadon, West Yorkshire. *Sedbergh History Society Archive*

The ex-Midland locomotive shed at Ingleton, seen here on 11th October, 1936 with (*below*), the ex-LNWR shed and turntable at Ingleton Thornton with Ingleton Midland station seen in the distance over the viaduct. The mineral branch is on the left just out of picture.

W.A. Camwell

Fowler 2-6-2T, No. 16 (ex-LMS), renumbered 40016, seen here on 1st May, 1948 standing at Ingleton with a train for Clapham. *W.A. Camwell*

Ingleton Midland as seen in 1968, with the Ingleton viaduct seen on the left. The station has now been demolished and over-built. *Author*

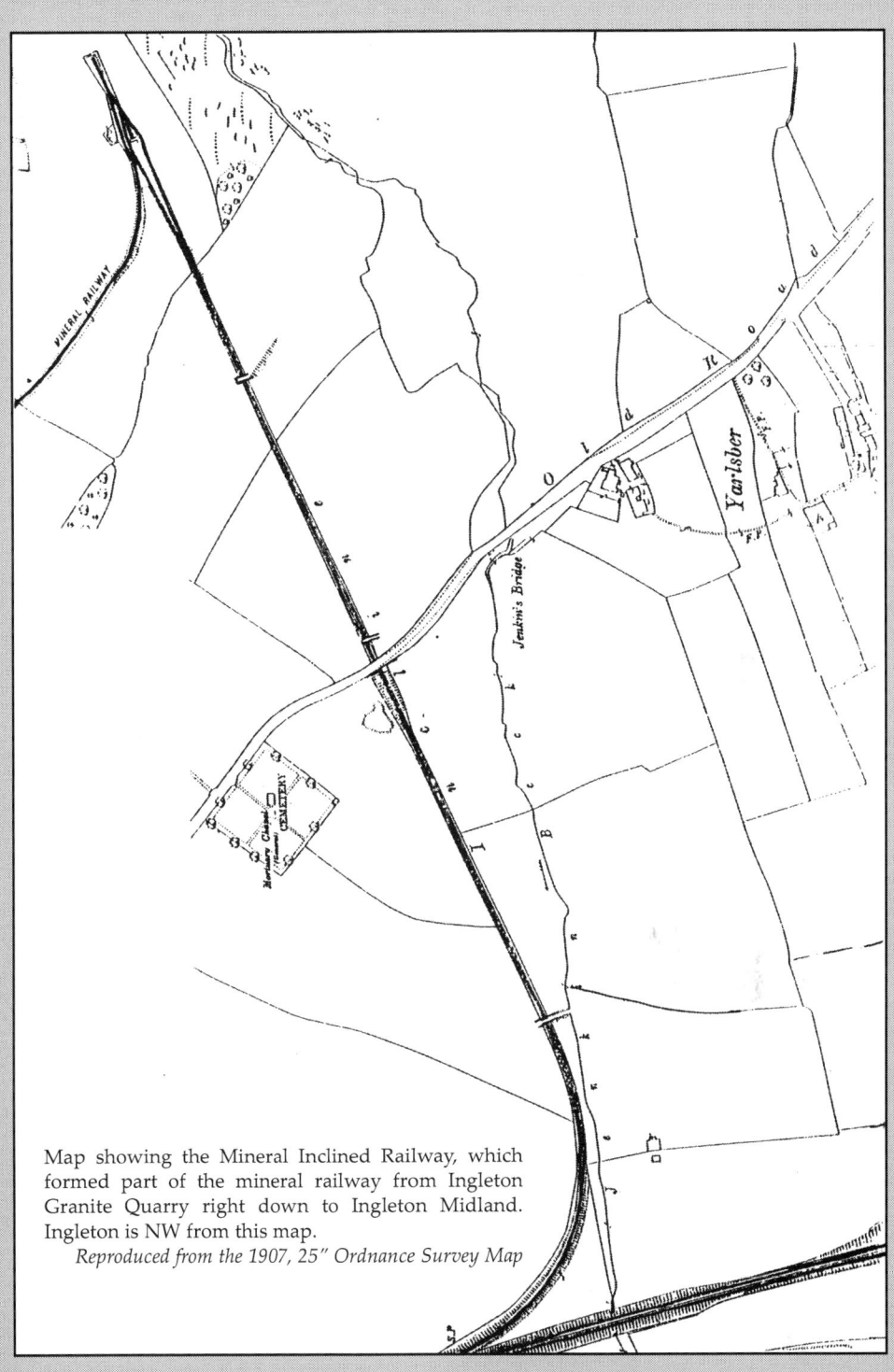

Map showing the Mineral Inclined Railway, which formed part of the mineral railway from Ingleton Granite Quarry right down to Ingleton Midland. Ingleton is NW from this map.
Reproduced from the 1907, 25" Ordnance Survey Map

The junction at Clapham, after the Lowgill Branch had been lifted in 1968, looking north-east from Clapham station footbridge. Note the derelict box and cattle dock.

H.B. Priestley

Clapham station, junction for Ingleton. Photographed at the turn of the century, it shows the timber and plaster mock Tudor style architecture. *Lens of Sutton*

Chapter Seven

Decline and Closure
1948 to 1967

1948

In spite of the prevailing circumstances, the line did manage to keep going for a time after nationalization.

Even so, what income there was came in the main from the passenger traffic and coal, with comparatively small quantities of general agricultural requisites being carried. In this period, coal traffic consisted of 200 tons each week distributed along the branch. This was made up as 50 tons for Ingleton, 60 tons for Kirkby Lonsdale and 90 tons for Sedbergh. Most of this coal came onto the branch from Tebay, having initially been transported by way of Wennington and Carnforth. The wagons allocated for the branch were then attached to a local goods train. These trains did carry some general merchandise as well but the large quantities of cattle food, fertilisers and lime, once brought in by rail were, by this time, being carried by road. This was because road transport had the advantages of being more economical and also convenient from the point of view of the 'once handling' principle in getting the commodities delivered 'directly to the door'.

The end is nigh
1950
A vital choice is made

It was during the early 1950s that the railway system in the north-west came under more intense careful scrutiny.

There was much speculation about the Midland (Settle to Carlisle) main line and the Ingleton Branch from Clapham to Lowgill. The point at issue involved establishing the more satisfactory through route from the West Riding to Carlisle. Ironically the matter was the previous situation in reverse; namely which route should be closed. The route through Skipton, Clapham and the Ingleton Branch had much to commend it because the track mileage to be maintained was considerably less than the line from Settle to Carlisle simply because traffic on the Ingleton route would join the West Coast Main Line at Lowgill.

For some time it appeared that the Ingleton Branch would probably be the route chosen and for a while it was included in a scheme to form part of a Freightliner route which would be equipped with colour light signalling. However, as in the past, the proposals to include it in a main line between the West Riding and Scotland and, assuming the possible diversion of 'The Thames Clyde' and 'Waverley' expresses along this route between London and Scotland, was not realized. The view was upheld that greater hardship would be caused to the many rural communities on the Settle and Carlisle route by closing it rather than closing the Ingleton Branch.

Once again the Ingleton Branch almost made the grade to become part of a main line link to Scotland but then failed to be included. The result was that plans were made for the gradual closure of the line. The sequence of events would soon become all too familiar on many of Britain's branch lines. First, the withdrawal of passenger services followed by the withdrawal of freight facilities and finally, after a period of semi-dereliction, the removal of the track.

Closure
A celebration – with a tinge of sadness

The last passenger train was scheduled to run on Saturday 30th January, 1954. Fortunately it was decided that the event would not pass unnoticed.

Lord and Lady Shuttleworth and Mr and Mrs Fulford invited a number of people to join them for a private party on board the train scheduled to leave Ingleton at 6.52 pm (the 6.42 pm from Clapham).

Many people boarded the train wearing Victorian costume and some of the ladies even wore mourning veils to indicate the sadness of the event. On this occasion, instead of the usual two carriages, there were five corridor coaches. All were full. To add something of deja vue to the ceremony, the Kirkby Lonsdale brass band joined the party, echoing the presence of a similar group of musicians when the line opened.

In addition to those who travelled on the train, hundreds turned out to see it pass and of the 150 people who bought tickets to travel, many did not do so but simply wanted to have them as souvenirs.

In light snow 'The Ingleton Coffee Pot', as the train was affectionately dubbed, set off for Lowgill. It was driven by Mr Jack Bird of Ingleton who had worked on the line for nearly 25 years. His fireman was Mr Jack Stobbart of Sedbergh. The locomotive selected for this memorable occasion was Fowler class '4MT' 2-6-4T No.42396; a Tebay engine.

Mr Conchie, who had worked on the branch for some 40 years, was operating the block system at Sedbergh and saw the train safely through. When it arrived at Lowgill, various ceremonies were performed.

Clapham station looking south-east with No. 40067 running around the 1.55 pm local service to Lowgill on 19th September, 1953. *H.B. Priestley*

An invitation to travel on the last train. Note: the use of the local name 'Lune Valley Line' right upto the end!

Lord & Lady Shuttleworth
Mr & Mrs Roger Fulford

At Home

6.45 p.m. to 9.15 p.m.

Saturday, January 30th

On the last train to bid farewell to the *Lune Valley Line*

Heated Private Coach   Supper   Brass Band
Depart Ingleton 6-52 p.m.
Return Ingleton 9-10 p.m.

R.S.V.P. to Leck Hall, Cowan Bridge, Carnforth.

The crew of the last passenger train on 30th January, 1954 and (*below*) the smokebox wreath of No. 42396.
Courtesy Westmorland Gazette

Mrs Fulford made a short speech from the footplate of the locomotive. She praised the staff of the line for all their hard work and then presented driver Bird with a laurel wreath which was placed on the front of the locomotive. Gifts were presented to the driver, fireman and guard. The brass band played to a large crowd and the members forming the private party were served with refreshments.

The train then set off for the return journey to Ingleton but was delayed for 30 minutes by fog.

Once back in Ingleton, the crowd gave a loud cheer, sang 'Auld Lang Syne' and the locomotive was put in the engine shed for the last time.

This sort of occasion would be repeated up and down the country many times in the following years.

After the passenger service ended, the daily freight continued to run as before, being run from Tebay shed and leaving Tebay at approximately 10.15 am. It travelled to Clapham and returned to Tebay during the afternoon. It left Ingleton at 2.10 pm but the times en route for the return varied according to the amount of shunting needed.

After February 1956 this freight service was reduced to three trains each week, these operating on Monday, Wednesday and Friday. Freight facilities ceased for Barbon on 2nd April, 1964 and then on Thursday 1st October of the same year all freight services were withdrawn with the exception of the Ingleton Thornton and Midland yards which continued to have a freight service from Clapham for a further five months.

School Specials

After the closure to general passenger services, special trains were run for the benefit of pupils at Sedbergh School, Casterton School, Cressbrook School and Kirkby Lonsdale School.

Originally Sedbergh and Casterton Schools ended terms on different dates so resulting in the need to run special trains on two days. This lack of any co-ordination lasted for some time but eventually the point was taken that running two sets of specials added considerably to the expense and so an arrangement was agreed whereby special trains ran on just one day.

The first train was for Sedbergh School only and this left Sedbergh at 7.00 am. It ran straight through to Carlisle for connections to Scotland. The second left Sedbergh at about 7.40 am. This train had through coaches for Leeds and stopped at Barbon where pupils from Casterton joined it and, in later years, it also stopped at Kirkby Lonsdale where pupils from Kirkby Lonsdale Grammar School joined the train. At Clapham the coaches of this train were attached to a Morcambe – Leeds train.

A further train left Barbon, where Casterton pupils boarded, at about 8.20 am. In later years this train started at Kirkby Lonsdale in order to allow pupils from Cressbrook School (which was situated at Kirkby Lonsdale) and also pupils from the Grammar School to join it. This train went on to stop at Sedbergh where pupils from the school could board. From there the train went to Lowgill where the locomotive ran round the train which then went forward to Preston. At this point a connection to Euston could be made.

At the beginning of the school term fewer special arrangements were made. The 10.40 am from Euston had two special coaches and stopped at Lowgill. These coaches were detached at this point and were then taken down the branch by a Tebay engine. This train went to Sedbergh only and after Lowgill station was closed on 7th March, 1960, the coaches were detached at Tebay. From the Carlisle end there were no special arrangements and those coming from this direction used normal services.

Eventually the need for these special trains declined as pupils were brought in by car. As a result, the practice was to run the 7.00 am special from Sedbergh at the end of term, to Tebay only. Eventually these special services were withdrawn altogether and the pupils who had to travel some distance by train were taken by bus to Oxenholme station to travel on from there.

After the freight services ceased the coal merchants operating from the rail depots on the line had no option but to receive their coal supplies by road. In spite of this, British Rail adopted a policy of imposing tolls on the entry of all roadborne fuels into its yards. This, understandably, was considered to be unfair by the various merchants involved as the circumstances which resulted in this outcome had been forced upon them by British Rail. Eventually British Rail was pressed to sell the yards and after lengthy negotiation, agreed to do so. At about the same time, Sedbergh station was sold to the former station master to be used as a private dwelling.

Some respite.......

Although, in effect, the line was completely closed, the track was kept in good repair in order that it could be used as a relief line, if so needed. It had proved to be of value in the very severe winter of 1962/63 when the

Kirkby Lonsdale brass band playing on the occasion of the last passenger train over the branch. How many of these men's predecessors played on the occasion of the first passenger train, one wonders? *Courtesy Westmorland Gazette*

A Stanier class '5MT' 4-6-0 waits by Clapham Junction signal box before going up the branch to retrieve a train of scrap wagons during the removal of the track. *F. Dean*

Settle-Carlisle line was completely blocked by deep snow for several weeks especially in the area around Dent.

During this period the branch was used by a considerable amount of diverted traffic, including 'The Thames Clyde Express'.

......and the end

By Spring 1967 it had been decided that it was uneconomical even to maintain the track and so the removal of this commenced during April. The work was carried out by T.W.Ward & Co. of Sheffield.

The up line was removed first and by the end of 1967 the track had gone.

The end really had come. This lost route to Scotland was now really lost – for ever.

The view from the site of the road bridge (Ingleton-Clapham Road) looking towards the west. Ingleton is in the background. The path of the inclined railway (*see map page 77*) which formed part of the mineral railway from the 'Ingleton Granite Quarry' (now ARC Roadstone) can be clearly seen following the wall and then sweeping round to the right towards Ingleton Midland. Photographed on the 6th May, 1989. *Author*

Chapter Eight

A Review of Motive Power on the Branch

By the time the Ingleton Branch opened in 1862, James Ramsbottom had replaced Francis Trevithick as the Chief Mechanical Engineer (CME) of the LNWR at Crewe and so it was Ramsbottom's engines that operated on the line. It was his 'Special DX' 0-6-0 class that was the first to be used and these remained a common sight up to the end of the 19th century.

Eventually tank engines were used for passenger services on the branch as these were more appropriate because the journeys which terminated at Ingleton and Lowgill necessitated the engine running round the train for the return journey (although there was a turntable at Ingleton). These were Tebay engines and the shed at Ingleton came under Tebay.

Following an alleged disagreement with Richard Moon, Ramsbottom stepped down and was followed by Francis Webb who became CME at Crewe in 1857. Consequently passenger services were usually hauled by Webb's 2-4-2 tank engines and both the 5ft 6in. and 4ft 6in. varieties were used. Of the former, No. 2126 is reported as being seen frequently on the branch; of the latter, No. 2541. In addition, Webb's 0-6-0 'Coal Engines' also put in frequent appearances.

After Webb came Whale who was made CME in 1903 but he only held the post for five years.

Bowen-Cooke took over in 1908 and some of his 4-6-2 super-heated tank locomotives spent their last days at Tebay acting as banking engines on Shap and these were occasionally reported as being seen on the branch. Bowen-Cooke stayed with the LNWR until 1919 and by this time changes were looming. The LNWR was planning an amalgamation with the Lancashire and Yorkshire Railway (L&Y) (a second attempt) which it hoped would take place in 1921 but these plans were overtaken by the Government's decision to go ahead with setting up four main railway companies. The LNWR passed into the LMSR group.

Soon after the LMS came into existence, Fowler became the CME in 1925 and until 1933 and his locomotives appeared on the branch. His '3MT' 2-6-2T class appeared (by now, it will be recalled, the line was seen as being from Lowgill to Clapham) and with the renumbering after nationalization, Nos. 40016, 40024 and 40070 became regulars. Just before the line closed to passenger services, Fowler's class '4MT' 2-6-4T locomotives had taken over. One of these locomotives, No. 42396 (as renumbered) was often in evidence and worked the last passenger service. This resulted in it being the last locomotive to be shedded at Ingleton. This class, based at Tebay, also did banking duties on Shap as well.

The motive power for through trains varied considerably over the years and the use of the line as a relief route for various reasons brought a wide variety of motive power.

An early service in this category was 'The Lake District Express'. This ran from Leeds but there was a connection from London. The Midland engine was taken off at Clapham and replaced by an LNWR locomotive which was one of Ramsbottom's 'Newton' or sometimes 'Jumbo' 2-4-0 classes.

Through freight in the early years was hauled by a locomotive of the 'Special DX' class and later by Webb's 'Coal Engines'. Much later, local goods were often handled by the tank engines and then by H.A. Ivatt's 2-6-0 class which took over some of the work. Towards the end the 'Bamber Bridge Goods' was usually in charge of a Stanier class '5MT' 4-6-0 or, occasionally, a Stanier class '8F' 2-8-0.

In addition to the regular services there were excursions which ran over the line, not least because it was noted for its scenic attraction. These were legion and no doubt many have gone unrecorded. Certainly in 1962 a 'special' called 'The Lincolnshire Poacher' used the line and was headed by a class 'V2' 2-6-2 No. 60870. There were also 'Ramblers' Specials' during the 1960s and these were usually operated by diesel multiple-units (dmus)

There were occasions, for example when the Settle and Carlisle line was impassable, but in other situations as well, when the branch was used as a relief line. This happened after the crash on the Settle and Carlisle in 1910 and a variety of Midland trains were diverted and used the branch for a time. Whilst it might be possible to speculate what the motive power might have been, there was, it seems, nobody around to make lists or record any details. There is a record of a Stanier 'Duchess' class Pacific using the branch in 1948. It was apparently being piloted and the reason for this diversion does not seem to have been given. One event that did get a lot of publicity was the extreme weather conditions in the area during the winter of 1962/3 when the Settle and Carlisle line was completely blocked by snow for a considerable period. A large variety of traffic came on to the branch and perhaps the most distinguished visitors were the Sulzer Type '4' diesels hauling 'The Thames- Clyde' express.

One of the last steam locomotives to use the branch was *Flying Scotsman* on a Carlisle-bound 'Special' in November 1965.

Bowen-Cooke 4-6-2T on a local Ingleton Branch train in 1927. Many of these engines finished their days at Tebay and consequently worked the branch, as well as banking on Shap.

J. McGowen

One of the earliest types of tank engine to work the Ingleton Branch was the Webb, 4 ft 6 in., 2-4-2T, No. 2514 seen here on the turntable at Ingleton, at the turn of the century.

Author's Collection

Ingleton Branch.

Stations.		WEEK DAYS.				
		a.m.	a.m.		p.m.	p.m.
Midland { Leeds	dep	5 35	8 0	...	10 42	3 50	...
Bradford	,,	5 50	8 30	...	10 48	3 52	...
Skipton	,,	7 7	9 35	...	11 40	4 43	...
Ingleton { Midland	arr	8 15	10 35	...	12 50	5 40	...
{ L. & N. W. { arr		8 22	10 40	...	12 57	5 47	...
{ dep		8 45	11 0	...	1 45	5 55	...
Kirkby Lonsdale	dep	8 55	11 10	...	1 55	6 5	...
Barbon	,,	9 0	11 20	...	2 3	6 15	...
Middleton	,,	9 6	11 27	...	2 10	6 22	...
Sedbergh	,,	9 13	11 38	...	2 18	6 30	...
Low Gill Junction	,,	9 22	11 50	...	2 28	6 40	...
Tebay	arr	9 30	12 0	...	2 38	6 50	...
Penrith	arr	11 28	1 0	...	4 10	8 0	...
Carlisle	,,	12 15	1 30	...	5 0	8 45	...
		a.m.	noon		p.m.	p.m.	
Oxenholme	arr	10 4	12 37	...	3 7	7 27	
Kendal	,,	10 20	12 50	...	3 20	7 35	
Lancaster	,,	10 50	1 30	...	3 46	8 17	
Preston	,,	11 3	2 30	...	4 24	9 15	
Manchester (Vic. L. & N. W.)	,,	12 40	4 35	...	6 0	10 45	
Liverpool (Lime Street)	,,	12 50		...	5 50	10 40	
Birmingham	,,	2 30	6 30	...	11 25	2 10	
LONDON (Euston)	,,	4 40	8 0	...	.	5 30	
		nght	a.m.	a.m.		a.m.	
LONDON (Euston)	dep	12 0	...	7 15	...	11 0	
Birmingham	,,	3 5	...	8 50	...	12 40	
Liverpool (Lime Street)	,,	...	6 0	10 45	...	4 10	
Manchester (Vic. L. & N. W.)	,,	1 20	5 55	10 50	...	4 15	
Preston	,,	6 5	8 5	12 45	...	5 25	
Lancaster	,,	6 35	9 5	1 40	...	5 55	
Kendal	,,	7 10	9 35	2 35	...	6 25	
Oxenholme	,,	7 18	9 58	2 42	...	6 35	
		a.m.	a.m.	p.m.		p.m.	
Carlisle	dep	...	8 40	1 40	...	5 45	...
Penrith	,,	...	9 10	2 10	...	6 25	
Tebay	dep	7 30	10 25	3 0	...	7 15	
Low Gill Junction	,,	7 45	10 35	3 13	...	7 25	
Sedbergh	,,	7 53	10 45	3 22	...	7 35	
Middleton	,,	8 1	10 52	3 29	...	7 43	
Barbon	,,	8 11	11 2	3 33	...	7 53	
Kirkby Lonsdale	,,	8 23	11 12	3 48	...	8 5	
Ingleton { L. & N. W. arr		8 32	11 25	4 0	...	8 15	
{ Midland { arr		8 35	11 30	4 5	...	...	
{ dep		8 40	12 10	6 35	...	...	
Midland { Skipton	arr	9 31	1 20	7 42	...	...	
Bradford	,,	10 10	2 40	8 35	...	...	
Leeds	,,	10 20	2 47	8 42	...	...	

Passengers from or to the Ingleton Branch change at Tebay or Low Gill Junction, according to the Service of Trains by which they travel.

The LNWR Passenger timetable for 1884.

The LNWR Passenger timetable for 1894.

INGLETON BRANCH.					Passengers to or from the Ingleton Branch change at Tebay or Low Gill Junction, according to the Service of Trains by which they travel.						
WEEK DAYS ONLY.	nght	a.m.	a.m.	p.m.	**WEEK DAYS ONLY.**		a.m.	a.m.	a.m.	p.m.	
LONDON (Euston) depart	12 0	10 10	...	...	Midland { Leeds	depart	...	5 55	8 5	11 0	3 35	...
Liverpool (Lime Street) ,,	...	6 10	1 55	3 55	Bradford	,,	...	5 55	8 32	11 0	3 25	...
(L. & Y.) ,,	2 40	6 10	2 25	4 10	Skipton	,,	...	7 0	9 29	11 53	4 27	...
Manchester (L. & N. W.) ,,	1 0	6 0	2 15	4 15	INGLETON { Midland .. depart		...	8 20	10 25	1 5	5 25	...
(L. & Y.) ,,	...	6 50	1 35	4 5	{ L. & N. W. arrive		...	8 25	10 30	1 8	5 30	...
Preston ,,	6 10	8 30	3 17	5 15	{ depart		...	8 45	10 35	1 40	6 10	...
Lancaster (Castle) ,,	6 38	9 0	3 45	5 43	Kirkby Lonsdale		...	8 55	10 43	1 50	6 18	...
Kendal ,,	7 10	9 46	4 10	6 21	Barbon		...	9 2	10 49	1 57	6 24	...
Low Gill arrive from South	7 40	10 19	...	6 54	Middleton		...	9 9	10 56	2 4	6 31	...
Tebay ,, ,,	...	...	4 45	...	Sedbergh		...	9 17	11 2	2 12	6 37	...
Carlisle depart	...	8 40	1 50	5 38	Low Gill Junction	arrive	...	9 26	11 10	2 21	6 45	...
Penrith ,,	...	9 9	2 30	6 15	Tebay	,,	...	9 35	11 18	2 30	...	...
Tebay arrive from North	...	9 42	3 14	6 55	Tebay	depart for North	...	10 27	12 6	2 56	7 2	...
Tebay depart	7 30	10 5	4 59	6 55	Penrith	arrive	...	11 5	12 29	3 33	7 39	...
Low Gill Junction ,,	7 43	10 22	4 58	7 12	Carlisle	,,	...	11 45	1 5	4 10	8 15	...
Sedbergh ,,	7 52	10 31	5 9	7 21	Tebay	depart for South	...	9 42	...	2 37	...	...
Middleton ,,	8 0	10 39	5 17	7 29	Low Gill	,, ,,	...	...	11 37	...	...	...
Barbon ,,	8 8	10 47	5 25	7 37	Kendal	arrive	...	10 15	12 14	3 16	7 40	...
Kirkby Lonsdale ,,	8 17	10 56	5 34	7 46	Lancaster (Castle)	,,	...	10 38	12 48	8 27	8 18	...
L. & N. W. arrive	8 26	11 5	5 43	7 55	Preston	,,	...	11 10	1 45	4 0	9 17	...
INGLETON { depart	8 28	11 7	5 45	...	Manchester (L. & Y.)	,,	...	12 27	3 20	5 8	10 37	...
{ Midland arrive	8 20	11 9	5 47	...	(L. & N. W.)	,,	...	12 34	3 0	6 17	11 13	...
Midland { Skipton arrive	9 34	1 5	7 45	...	Liverpool (L. & Y.)	,,	...	12 25	2 53	5 30	11 6	...
Bradford ,,	10 20	2A 26	8 33	...	(Lime Street)	,,	...	12 8	3 0	4 10	11 5	...
Leeds ,,	10 22	2 46	8 45	...	LONDON (Euston)	,,	...	4 15	6 45	10 15	3 50	...

B—First and Third Class only.
A—Arrives Bradford 2.5 p.m. on Saturdays.

TEBAY and INGLETON (1st and 3rd class).—London and North Western.

Bradshaw's timetable for April 1910.
Bradshaw's timetable for July 1922.

TEBAY, INGLETON, and CLAPHAM

Bradshaw's timetable for July 1938.
Bradshaw's timetable for May 1948.

Table 198 — TEBAY, INGLETON, and CLAPHAM

Passengers to or from the Ingleton Branch change at Tebay or Low Gill, according to the service of trains by which they travel.

The remains of the high bridge which took the mineral railway from Meal Bank Quarry to Ingleton Thornton over the entrance to the Ingleton walks. Photographed in May 1989.

Author

The old tunnel entrance to Meal Bank Quarry now bricked up (May 1989).   *Author*

Chapter Nine

After Closure

The Lowgill and Ingleton viaducts, together with the Rawthey (Jackdaw) and Lune (Waterside) viaducts, with the small viaduct at Leck, still remain.

Ingleton, Waterside and Lowgill viaducts are 'listed' buildings under the 'Planning (Listed Buildings and Conservation Areas) Act. Lowgill viaduct was given this status on 21st February, 1989 and Ingleton, similarly, on 23rd November, 1988. Waterside, which straggles two local councils, was listed on the Firbank section on 14th June, 1984 and in the Sedbergh section on 18th October, 1999. The Rawthey viaduct is not listed but it carries a gas main (which means it out of bounds to the public) and in that sense, therefore, remains in use.

In 1993 it was reported that a conservationist had come up with a scheme 'to breathe new life into a disused Sedbergh viaduct by parking a Victorian-looking train on the structure and using it as a tourist attraction'. The viaduct in question was the Waterside viaduct and the plan was to put in place on this viaduct an engine, together with three carriages. Each carriages would provide a holiday let of 500 square feet. A feasibility study was to be carried out but the project never materialized. At about this time the British Rail Property Board was also attempting to sell off to preservation groups other viaducts at what was described as 'peppercorn prices' (£1 each had been suggested) together with the offer of £10,000 towards upkeep. Given that the arrangement was to keep the structures in a state of good preservation in perpetuity, it is probably no surprise that there were no takers!

It was therefore left to the British Railways Board (BRB) to take care of these listed viaducts and carry out routine maintenance checks. Subsequently, in 2007, the BRB (Residuary) arranged for extensive restoration work on the Waterside viaduct. The work was contracted out to Raynesway Construction and cost £600,000. Unlike the early days when the viaduct was originally built, this time a host of agencies had to be consulted first. The forefront were the Yorkshire Dales National Park Authority and South Lakeland District Council who in turn looked to English Heritage, the Victorian Society, the Ancient Monuments Society along with others. When all the initial procedures were completed, the Lune Valley once again echoed to the sound of work on the line – or at least one of the viaducts on it. The sounds, though, were very different. Certainly there were no horses, just the rumble of machinery. No accidents, either, this time, as there had been on the original building works. Safety measures were paramount; a large section of scaffolding was erected which was visible when taking the road up to Firbank and special cradles were used to reach sections of the arches. The work, started in the early part of the year, was completed in May. The viaduct looked resplendent (and remains so) especially with the new coat of black paint on the central metal arch.

And of the rest...

Whilst a number of road bridges have been demolished to allow for improvements to the road system, a number still remain including the one on the Kirkby Lonsdale to Sedbergh Road on the approach towards Middleton. There are also bridges in places where tracks crossed the fells. Both Ingleton stations have been razed to the ground and at Lowgill there is little, other than the viaduct, to suggest there was once a junction here. Barbon station, too, has been demolished and the site overbuilt. There are a number of places where the former trackbed is easy to discern and some sections along which it is possible to walk.

At Ingleton, the path of the line used for the Meal Bank quarry workings can still be traced. The quarry area is used for parking but the tunnel entrance is still clearly visible on the west side although it has been bricked up. The centre sections of the bridges have been removed but visitors to the walks, which are still very popular, pass between the lofty columns of one of them. A section of the high embankment has been removed to provide additional parking space.

Evidence of the mineral line to the other quarry also remains. The bridge carrying the Ingleton to Clapham road has been filled in but the supporting girders are still visible. On the quarry side of this bridge, stone retaining walls lining a short cutting are very much in evidence. The path of the trackbed can be seen in a number of places.

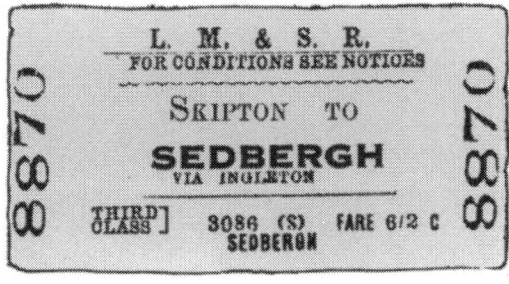

Appendix One

Bills affecting the Ingleton Branch

1846	NWR	Bill to build a new line of railway
1846 and 1848	NWR	For deviations
1852	NWR	Bill for extension of time to build the Orton Branch
1856	NWR	Bill for Tebay extension
1857	NWR	Bill for Ingleton to Tebay line
1857	L & C	Bill for the Ingleton to Lowgill line
1858	L & C	Bill for deviations at Lowgill Junction

INGLETON BRANCH.					
Distance from Low Gill. m.		m.	Rising or Falling towards Ingleton.	Gradient.	Between.
0	to	0⅛	Falling	1 in 777	Low Gill and Sedbergh.
0⅛	to	0¼	,, ...	1 in 220	,, ,, ,,
0¼	to	4⅛	,, ...	1 in 100	,, ,, ,,
4⅛	to	4¼	,, ...	1 in 200	,, and Middleton.
4¼	to	4⅞	,, ...	1 in 100	Sedbergh ,, ,,
4⅞	to	5	Level	Level......	,, ,, ,,
5	to	6	Rising	1 in 480	,, ,, ,,
6	to	6¾	Level	Level ...	,, ,, ,,
6¾	to	7⅞	Falling......	1 in 200	,, and Barbon.
7⅞	to	8⅜	Level	Level ...	Middleton ,, ,,
8⅜	to	9⅜	Falling......	1 in 250	,, ,, ,,
9⅜	to	10	Rising	1 in 330	,, ,, ,,
10	to	10½	Level	Level ...	,, ,, Kirkby Lonsdale.
10½	to	11⅞	Rising	1 in 150	Barbon and ,, ,,
11⅞	to	12¼	,, ...	1 in 500	,, ,, ,, ,,
12¼	to	12½	Level	Level ...	,, ,, ,, ,,
12½	to	13⅜	Falling......	1 in 120	,, ,, ,, ,,
13⅜	to	13¾	Level	Level ...	,, ,, ,, ,,
13¾	to	14⅛	Falling......	1 in 200	Kirkby Lonsdale and Ingleton.
14⅛	to	15⅜	Rising	1 in 140	,, ,, ,, ,,
15⅜	to	15⅞	,, ...	1 in 100	,, ,, ,, ,,
15⅞	to	16	,, ...	1 in 250	,, ,, ,, ,,
16	to	17	,, ...	1 in 140	,, ,, ,, ,,
17	to	18	,, ...	1 in 1200	,, ,, ,, ,,
18	to	end	,, ...	1 in 250	,, ,, ,, ,,

Table of gradients for the Ingleton Branch.

Appendix Two

Some Significant Dates in the History of the Ingleton Branch

1857	L & C Bill to build branch receives Parliamentary assent
1858	Summer. W.A.Sanders cuts the first sod
	November. First fatal accident occurs
1859	4th January. W.A.Sanders lays the foundation stone of the Lowgill viaduct
	4th March. Work recommenced in building the Ingleton viaduct, (the NWR had made a start)
1860	18th May. D. Campbell, the Resident Engineer, fixes the final keystone of the Ingleton viaduct
1861	16th September. The line opens
1917	Ingleton Thornton is closed
1931	Middleton (-on-Lune) station is closed
1954	Passenger services withdrawn
1956	March. Freight services reduced to three trains each week, Monday, Wednesday and Friday
1964	2nd April. Barbon station and yard closed
	1st October. All freight services withdrawn. Ingleton to Clapham freight remains for five further months
1967	Track removed

The elegant lines of Errington's bridges can be clearly seen in this view which shows the old Kirkby Lonsdale to Dent road overbridge. This was fairly typical of the bridge design on the branch. *Author*

A fine view of the 11-arch Ingleton viaduct, looking north. *Author*

Waterside viaduct, looking east, seen here after track removal. Note the centre span is similar to the Rawthey viaduct span. *Author*

The beautiful curved Lowgill viaduct as seen (*above*) in an old postcard at the turn of the century and (*below*) looking north after track removal.   *Author*

Appendix Three

Bridges and Viaducts

The line had 77 bridges, excluding the large viaducts at Ingleton and Lowgill, the small five-arch viaduct at Leck and the bridges over the River Lune and the River Rawthey.

The Ingleton viaduct
    Spans the Greta Gorge
    11 arches each with a span of 57 feet [17m]*
    Total length 800 feet [244m]
    Greatest height above the River Greta, 80 feet [24m]
    Built of white sandstone quarried at Bentham
    Built without loss of life or limb.
    Grade II listed 23rd November, 1988

The Rawthey viaduct   (local name sometimes used, Jackdaw viaduct.)
    Spans the River Rawthey
    Single span (metal arch) of 120 feet [37m]
    Set at 38° to the line of the track
    Height above the Rawthey, 53 feet [16m]
    Built of Penrith Stone
    (Not listed)

The Lune (or Waterside) viaduct
    Spans the River Lune
    6 arches and a centre span similar to the one on the Rawthey viaduct
    Total length 530 feet [162m]
    Height above the River Lune 100 feet [30m]
    Built of Penrith Stone
    Grade II listed Firbank PC 14th June, 1984, Sedbergh PC 18th October, 1999

The Lowgill (or Dillicar) viaduct
    Spans the Dillicar Beck
    11 arches each with a span of 45 feet [14m]
    Height above the beck, 90 feet [27m]
    Built of Penrith Stone
    Special ceremony for laying the foundation stone on 4th January, 1859
    Grade II listed 21st February, 1989

* Metric units given to the nearest whole number.

Stations

The Ingleton Branch
Ingleton Thornton
Kirkby Lonsdale
Barbon
Middleton (on-Lune)
Sedbergh
Low Gill (This form of the name was often used by the railway companies)

To these were added after the 1923 Grouping
Clapham
Ingleton Midland

The branch had one level crossing which adjoined Barbon station.

A bridge at the site of Ingleton Thornton station. The mounds of earth show where the platforms used to be.   *Author*

The Rawthey or Jackdaw viaduct which gracefully spans the River Rawthey. *Author*

The Midland Railway's station at Ingleton. *John Alsop Collection.*

Lune viaduct under scaffolding. *Graeme Bickerdike/Four by Three*

Sources

Minutes of Directors and shareholders meetings for the following companies:
- The Lancaster and Carlisle
- The North Western
- The London and North Western
- The Great Northern
- The Midland

The various Bills with plans deposited for presentation to Parliament and subsequent Acts (where appropriate).

Minutes of the meetings of the Lunesdale Agricultural Association for 24th September, 1859

The Westmorland Gazette
The Lancaster Guardian
The Derbyshire Advertiser and Journal
Timetables, various from 1862 – 1954

Cassells Official Guide to the LNWR (1892 Edition)
Humphries, Muriel, *A History of the Ingleton Waterfalls Walk*
Green Vigour, Julia, *Recollections of Sedbergh School and Town in Early Victorian Time*
Milne, G., *Ingleton Memories*
Milner's Guide to Railways, Coaches and Steamers in the North of England

Locations

The Public Records Office at Kew (now National Archives)
The Parliamentary Archives, House of Lords
The Cumbria Record Office Kendal (Formerly Westmorland County Archives Office, Kendal)
The County Archives Office at Wakefield.
The Records Office at Wakefield
The Sedbergh History Society Archive

Acknowledgements

Much of the material in Chapter five and subsequent chapters came from recollections of people still living at the time when the first edition was written. Back in those days, nearly 50 years ago, there were many people who could remember the line and were happy to share their memories of it. I was (and still am) grateful for the help of the late Mr Jack Dawson who used and then owned the coal yard at Sedbergh station; also to the late Mr Raymond Noddle who was British Rail inspector at Oxenholme and sought information from several of his colleagues on my behalf. The late Mrs Mary Udale had a wealth of memories. Her family moved to Sedbergh from the family home in Sheffield and at the age of 70+ when the first edition was being written, could recall tales of trips by her family when they travelled between Sedbergh and Sheffield which virtually went back to the time the line opened in 1862!

I am also indebted to Mr J.J.Wilson and Mr J. Slinger, both of Ingleton, who, whilst carrying out the revision in readiness for the second edition, provided me with a wealth of first-hand information about the quarries and mines at Ingleton. Mr Wilson recounted how his grandfather, who lived at the foot of Ingleborough, used to collect his stock of coal for winter in the manner described in the text.

Thanks, also, to the staffs of the various Archives and Records Offices for their help and guidance, in particular, Mr Simon Gough, the Archives Officer at the Parliamentary Archives at the House of Lords and, also, Diane Elphick and Elspeth Griffiths at Sedbergh History Society Archive.

A dmu entering Sedbergh station from the south on one of the many ramblers specials. Seen here on 16th June, 1963. *J.R. Sugden*